default Christianity

seeking *first* the kingdom of God in a world of distractions

NATHANAEL EGGER

default Christianity: seeking first the kingdom of God in a world of distractions

Copyright 2012 by Nathanael Egger

ISBN: 0615677525

ISBN 13: 9780615677521

Cover design by Christopher Auyeung (topherky.com)

Scripture quotations, unless otherwise indicated, are taken from *The Holy Bible: New International Version.* Grand Rapids, MI: Zondervan, 1984. Electronic version available from Logos Bible Software 4.

So do not worry, saying, "What shall we eat?" or "What shall we drink?" or "What shall we wear?" For the pagans run after all these things, and your heavenly Father knows that you need them. But seek first his kingdom and his righteousness, and all these things will be given to you as well.

—*Matthew 6:31–33*

For my darling Kristen Virginia,
who is my second greatest treasure—
happily below the King,
yet herself without compare.

Contents

Acknowledgements

This book is truly a product of the body of Christ. I have been thoroughly blessed by all the folks, in my local body and beyond, who have eagerly wrestled with me through the practical implications of putting God's kingdom first. Though this list is not exhaustive, I would like to thank a few of those folks specifically.

To begin, I owe my wife a great debt for not only allowing me to dedicate a tremendous amount of time to this book (on top of an already full work schedule) but for cheering me on along the way. Without her unwavering support, this would never have gotten off the ground. Thank you, darling. I look forward to you finally getting to read it for yourself.

Also, I want to acknowledge the support of Eric Russ, my pastor and friend, who first approached me with the idea of writing a book and has been a vocal fan through the entire process. Thank you, friend. If I ever recover from this book, maybe we can finally write one together.

Thank you also to my original "editors," including my brother Andy and my extended family in Christ, Nick, Caleb, and Sneha. Your insights were pivotal to the tone and direction of the book. The same is true for all the other readers and editors that have followed: Matthew and Betty, Alvin, Stephanie, Lee, Mark, Ann, Jonathan, and my father-in-law, Steve. Thank you for generously giving of yourselves and for setting me straight time and time again.

Finally, thank you to the rest of the body and pastors of Mack Avenue Community Church for providing the resources needed to make this book a reality.

A Note to the Reader

This is a book for ordinary folks who want to think and live as ordinary Christians for God. I am not a pastor or theologian or even a gifted writer, and I do not pretend to offer you anything new in this book. Still I recommend its truth to you. Yes, it is old and well-worn. Yes, it is hard to stomach at times. But it is drawn from the wells of Scripture, and thus this truth is life, welling up with joy and spilling over into eternity.

We were created to put God first in every part of our lives. That is the truth I want to explore with you. When we do put God first, we are thinking and acting as ordinary subjects of the kingdom of God. We are Christians living out default Christianity, which is to say, our fundamental and normative mode of operation.[1] On the other hand, when we put other things or people next to God in first place, or ahead of him, we are living as sinners and traitors to the one true King.

While the idea of putting God first sounds simple enough, it has taken me the better part of fifteen years of pursuing God in earnest to realize just how practical the idea is. Over that time I

---

[1] If you look in a dictionary for the definition of "default," you may note, as I did, that the first several definitions have to do with the failure to perform an obligation. This is most certainly not the sense in which I use default. Instead, I use it in the sense of "a selection made...automatically or without active consideration" (*Merriam-Webster's Collegiate Dictionary* [Springfield, MA: Merriam-Webster, Inc., 2003]). In this book, the word "default" represents the unspoken values that drive our daily life. While they do not provide active or conscious input, our values nevertheless guide our decisions about how to spend our time, energy, talents, and material resources. They are the parameters by which we engage the world around us.

have moved in and out of various Christian circles, read the Bible cover to cover several times, been discipled by multiple godly men, listened to hundreds of sermons, read dozens of Christian books with solid biblical teaching, and talked with many other professing believers.

What I learned is that "simple" does not mean "easy." We are too quickly distracted for it to be easy, and as fallen humans, putting God first is literally the last thing we want to (or can) do. This is why, even as professing Christians, we often go about our everyday lives without much, if any, conscious thought for God. It is also why we are content—again, even among professing Christians— to maintain such widely varying thoughts about our purpose and what values are most important in this world.

From the conversations I have had, it seems that most of us live life largely by feel. By that, I mean we look at all the possible choices, weigh the pros and cons, and ultimately go with what feels right. Often we do not take time to explore what makes something "feel right." I know that I did not. I just assumed that if I was reading my Bible and praying that I was going to be making godly decisions.

It was not until I began having to explain my decision to live with my wife and our family in one of the many struggling neighborhoods of Detroit that I really took time to explore the assumptions and values that shape my own thinking. During that process I went back to God's Word, the Bible, to find out not just what believers are called to but how we are taught to think and measure our decisions.

Scripture has plenty to say about right thinking and right living. There are hundreds of black-and-white moral commands with clear application. At the same time, a lot is left unsaid or unspecified. Most of life seems to fall into what can be thought of as gray or nonmoral and ill-defined areas in which Christians can disagree and still be Christians.

Where is that line between temptation and sin, for instance, or what does it mean to live godly lives rather than moral ones that are devoid of sin? What does "glorifying God and enjoying him forever"[2] look like now, in the Monday-through-Saturday grind of life? How do I practically seek first God's kingdom in every decision? (For example: Should I marry? If so, whom? What kind of career should I pursue? Where should I live or go to school? How should I spend my money or time?)

My problem was that I was never taught what to do with gray areas or how to encourage Christians who do not agree with me in the specifics of gray areas. While in theory, Scripture was the common standard for Christians, I (and almost everyone I was in conversation with) tended to emphasize certain parts of Scripture at the expense of other parts. In doing so, I not only sacrificed the integrity of Scripture but also allowed my disagreements to turn into divisions and hostility.

As I read Scripture, though, I began to recognize a motif that seemed to run from Genesis to Revelation. Whether it was the created order, the first commandment, the principle of tithing, God's jealous guard of Israel's attention, or Jesus's call to seek first the kingdom of God, everything seemed to point to God's desire to be preeminent, or of first importance, in the hearts, minds, and lives of his people. In other words, before we think about anything else (even the things most vital to our survival, like food, clothing, and shelter) we consider how our actions add or detract from God's kingdom.

Then, two ideas came together. First, God's kingdom is about his reign and rule in the hearts of people. Second, living in God's kingdom, under his rule, means recovering our created purpose of being image bearers (living out godliness) who, through God's power, fill the earth with other image bearers (make disciples).

Here is where the simple rule of "seeking first God's kingdom" gets very practical. It means structuring our lives (time, resources, location, career, family, and so forth) in such a way that encourages

---

[2]Westminster Shorter Catechism Question 1: What is the chief end of man? Answer: Man's chief end is to glorify God and enjoy him forever (http://www.reformed.org/documents/WSC.html, access date July 8, 2012).

personal godliness (putting to death sin and putting on Christlike fruits of the Spirit) *and* that encourages us to make disciples of others (being exposed to the physical and spiritual needs of our neighbors, inviting nonbelievers to experience God in word and deed, and teaching believers to obey everything Jesus commanded). Anything that distracts us from that should be cut off or put to death. Anything that adds to that effort should be retained or sought out.

When I began to talk with other Christians about this idea, I got some interesting reactions. Most folks had never thought of life that way. They had never thought of having a single reference point for measuring their life. It was always God and a handful of other equally important things like family, career, education, safety, or comfort.

Discovering that duplicity made us all a little defensive and uncomfortable at first. However, many pushed through that, and though it seemed paradoxical at the start, we eventually discovered that giving God everything is much easier than continuing on in halfhearted duplicity, juggling the world's reference points right along with King Jesus.

The God-first-and-alone idea also exposed many hidden idols in myself and in those I talked about it with. With the ambiguity gone, our misplaced values were easy to see. For example, one of the more interesting patterns that arose was the tendency toward imbalance among service-oriented or theology-oriented Christians. By recognizing the inseparable nature of the physical and spiritual elements within the kingdom of God, much of this imbalance was done away with.

So I offer you and every other professing Christian one reference point to fix our eyes on and mark our progress by: God's rule in the hearts of humans. Though nothing about the kingdom-first teaching is new or extraordinary, we are fallen people and can always stand to be reminded to fix our eyes on King Jesus and make his lordship in our lives our number-one priority.

Thank you for joining me. My vantage point is not that of one who has arrived at the journey's end, but simply that of another traveler. Learning to seek *first* the kingdom has brought refreshing clarity, balance, and depth to my walk with Christ. While I continue to obey the black-and-white commands of Scripture, the bulk of life has opened up for bold and creative service to the King. The gray areas are no longer safe hiding places for my idols but opportunities for cultivating godliness.

I pray that God might use this work to connect some of the same dots that he, through his Word and his people, has been connecting for me over the past fifteen years. Every word is born out of my own struggle to put to death my earthly nature and to take hold of life in Christ. The sins I attack are my own, and the deeds I exhort you to are the same ones I find so lacking in my own life.

Please do not read this book with the goal of finding a list of specific and complete answers regarding right thinking or right living. I cannot give you that list. I do not think that anyone can, for there are endless possibilities. Even with the best intentions, attempts at generating one-size-fits-all applications for the specific details of the kingdom life tend to lead to us into crippling imbalances.

God's rule is the datum from which life began and continues to flow most naturally. I offer it to you with the hope that you will neither be paralyzed by the gray areas of life nor indifferent to their kingdom potential, as I have been for too long. If you have not already, I hope that you will begin the lifelong process of learning to make every opportunity a chance to answer the Christian's default calling to seek first the kingdom of God in a world of distractions.

As with any book, there are assumptions I, the writer, hold that shape the tone and content of this work. Many of these assumptions you will undoubtedly pick up as you read along. There are others, however, that I would like to share with you now, at the beginning, to avoid any unnecessary confusion. Along with these theological assumptions, I have also included a few warnings as to peculiarities of my style and content that I hope will better prepare you to receive what this book has to offer.

Theological Assumptions (or Tenants)

- *Scripture is the highest authority.* I most definitely am not. Nor is your friend or pastor or favorite Christian author. Scripture is not the only authority, but it is the one with the final say on who God is and what it means to be a person under his rule.[3] Test everything I say according to God's Word.[4] I should not be adding anything to or detracting anything from God's Word.[5] If what I say agrees with God's Word and exalts Jesus as the Christ, then take it to heart. Otherwise, throw it away and gently but firmly rebuke me.[6]

- *Our calling is overarching and general with little, if any, specific direction.* While we can choose to wait around for all manner of signs and omens to determine God's particular will for our particular situation, he has made it plain in the Bible what he expects of every Christian. Those who received specific callings in Scripture to certain places or activities were rare, spread out over more than fifteen hundred years. Moreover, when these specific callings did occur, they did not replace the primary and common call to put God first, but informed and augmented it.[7] Rather than relying on omens, dreams, or fleeces to make decisions, we can open our Bibles and get to know our God.[8] When we put him first, the specific details have a way of taking care of themselves.

---

[3]God does reveal himself to us through other means, such as creation (Romans 1:20) and directly through his Spirit (Matthew 10:20; John 14:25–26). He also explicitly instruct us to submit to other lesser authorities such as our church leaders and elders (Hebrews 13:7, 17) and even non-Christian government officials (Romans 13:1–7; 1 Peter 2:13–17) so long as those authorities do not prevent us from sharing the good news of salvation in Christ (Acts 4:18–20).

[4]Galatians 1:8; 1 John 4:1–3; 2 John 10; 1 Thessalonians 5:21.

[5]Deuteronomy 12:32; Revelation 22:18–19.

[6]Timothy 2:25.

[7]For example, consider the call of Abram (Genesis 12:1–3) who was called to a specific land as part of a much larger plan to bring God's rule, through Jesus, to "all peoples on the earth."

[8]For more on discerning God's will, I recommend reading *Just Do Something* by Kevin DeYoung (Chicago, IL: Moody, 2009).

- *God's will is spoken of on multiple levels in Scripture, in seemingly contradictory ways.* God reigns sovereignly over every part of his creation, and in this context, God's will is spoken of as one of *decree.* What he commands happens every time without exception. This is the will spoken of in Proverbs 19:21, among other passages, which reads, "Many are the plans in a man's heart, but it is the Lord's purpose that prevails." God's accomplishes his will of decree in spite of and even through our independent acts of volition.[9] Yet God also has a will of *desire*, which refers to the explicit and implicit commands found in Scripture, summed up by Jesus in the two commands to love God and love our neighbor.[10] These serve as a description of how we can think and act in ways that please God. Unlike God's will of decree, his will of desire is something that we can choose to disobey, or thwart, and we will be held responsible for that choice.

- *A healthy biblical tension exists between man's responsibility and God's sovereignty.* As theologian J. I. Packer puts it, "The fact of free agency[11] confronts us with mystery…God's control over our free, self-determined activities is as complete as it is over anything else, and how this can be we do not know."[12] In other words, humans make decisions all the time, and we will be held responsible for whether these are godly or otherwise. This is why exhortations in Scripture, and in this book, are directed at us as individuals. Yet at the very same time, and without doing away with our responsibility, God is still accomplishing his sovereign will of decree in and through each of our decisions.

- *There is an eternal difference between being a professing Christian and a true Christian.* As Scripture reads, "Not everyone who says to me, 'Lord, Lord,' will enter the kingdom of

---

[9]Genesis 50:19–20; Judges 14:3–4; Isaiah 10:5–7; John 11:49–52.

[10]Matthew 27:37–40.

[11]J I. Packer, *Concise Theology* (Wheaton, IL: Tyndale House, 1995). Packer defines "free agency" as the ability of humans to make choices "in the light of their sense of right and wrong and the inclinations they feel." This is in contrast to free will, which he defines as "the ability to choose *all* the moral options that a situations offers" (emphasis added).

[12]Packer *Concise Theology.*

heaven, but only he who does the will of my Father who is in heaven. Many will say to me on that day, 'Lord, Lord, did we not prophesy in your name, and in your name drive out demons and perform many miracles?' Then I will tell them plainly, 'I never knew you. Away from me, you evildoers!'"[13] Sometimes we can see the difference easily between an unbeliever and a believer by examining the fruits of their lives, and other times it is much harder to discern.[14] I have no intention of discerning between who is "in" and who is "out," but to hold all professing Christians to the standard that we are claiming by saying "Lord, Lord" to Jesus Christ.

Particularities of this Book

- *This is a hard book to read.* From the response I have received, it seems the difficulty is mostly related to content. The call of Christ to each of us would-be followers is the call to die to ourselves, that we may find true and abundant life in him. Dying is hard, in part because it hurts. There is no way around that. Dying is also hard because it takes much Holy Spirit–motivated effort, usually expended over many years, to see his fruit on every branch of your life. If your desire is to see this book aid in your transformation into a kingdom-first disciple, then please count the cost. Much time, prayer, mediation, and discussion will be required for God's truth to renew your mind and bear fruit in your daily life.
- *There are many questions and possible applications.* Please consider them *all*. When I am in a hurry, my tendency is to skip past questions and disregard study guides at the end of books. However, I urge you to give the questions a chance to sink in so that you can begin to apply what you are learning

---

[13]Matthew 7:21–23.
[14]Matthew 7:15–20.

along the way. If you become overwhelmed by applications, my advice is to slow down, not skip ahead. There are no prizes for finishing this book quickly, but Scripture has much to offer those who take to heart the call to seek first the kingdom in everything.

- *This book is a survey, not an in-depth study.* While the call to follow Christ is life transforming, it is also relatively simple. As with any discussion of the Christian life, however, big and controversial topics do come up in this book. Where they do, I have done my best to stay true to Scripture and not overstep its level of clarity. The result is that some issues may be explained and discussed to your satisfaction, but others will leave you with questions. Please feel free to explore these further on your own. Where helpful, I have tried to include references to passages in Scripture, as well as other books and sermons that I have benefited from in the past.

- *Some words are used synonymously and interchangeably.* I mention this because so often we use these words in separate contexts and may have never connected them in our minds before. For example, in this book, the following words will be used interchangeably: believer, disciple, Christian, follower, and kingdom subject. Similarly, the following terms describing God's kingdom on earth will be used interchangeably: body of Christ, church, community of believers, and disciples. Although this may diminish some of the theological nuances of each word or phrase, they seem to have enough overlap to justify using them synonymously in this book.

- *A fair amount of quotes, references, and footnotes are used.* That is intentional. While I could have done more rewording and adaptation of the passages from other sources to make the quotes go away (and the book more readable), I wanted it to be abundantly clear that the thoughts in this book are not new. They have been in Scripture for thousands of years and have been faithfully reiterated by God's people since the canon of Scripture was closed. For my part, I am merely standing in that long line of folks who brought to the surface, in their own day and cultural context, the good news of death to self and life in Christ

Introduction

Think about your how your day went today. Where did you wake up? What did you eat? What did you wear? What did you do? Where did you go? With whom did you interact? How did you spend your time, your money, and your energy?

Now think about why you woke up where you woke up and ate what you ate and did what you did today? Why a house rather than an apartment, or vise versa? Why a hotel? Why eat oatmeal rather than eggs and bacon? Why coffee instead of soda or water? Why did you buy that specific shirt or book, chair or car? Why did you choose your career or your workplace? Why do you spend your time with these people instead of those people, or here not there?

Your answer to each of these questions may have multiple levels. For example, you may say that you live in an apartment because it is close to your job. And the reason you want to live close to your job is because you would rather spend time with friends than commuting to and from work. And the reason you like to spend time with your friends is because they make you feel valued.

Eventually, if you take that idea out far enough, you will reach what I call an "ultimate why," or fundamental value, that works both on a conscious level and, perhaps what is more important, on a structural level, behind the scenes, to guide your daily actions. This book is about getting to the ultimate whys in your life and replacing them with the one championed repeatedly in Scripture, which is to build God's kingdom.[15]

My proposal is simple. If the fundamental reason you think what you think, say what you say, and do what you do is not to build God's kingdom, than you have a very real problem on your hands—you are not a true Christian. The same is true for me and for every human. God wants to be our defining purpose. He demands preeminence, or first importance, in our lives. He will settle for nothing less from his people. Yet less is what we so often settle for. This is true, even among those who call themselves Christians and have done so for years.

Our problem frequently starts when we try to add Jesus onto our lives as they currently exist. Though much change may occur on the surface of our lives, little if any space in our hearts is cleared of old values (and gods) to make room for Jesus. Instead, we are often guilty of adding him onto our lives much like we would an ornament, while continuing to chase after whatever we were before we met him. As pastor and author A. W. Tozer explained, this leaves professing Christians with a predicament:

> *The evil habit of seeking God-and effectively prevents us from finding God in full revelation. In the "and" lies our great woe. If we omit the "and" we shall soon find God, and in Him we shall find that for which we have all our lives been secretly longing.*[16]

Despite all the warnings in Scripture and of faithful Christians through history, our fleshly tendency is still to treat Jesus as a god among gods. We want to seek him *and* everything we wanted long before we met him, whether that is health, purpose, morals, family, wealth, community, safety, or any number of other things that we

---

[15]God's kingdom exists only in the hearts of his singularly devoted disciples who have submitted themselves to follow his rule, or will of desire. Since, as we will soon see, we are all commanded to encourage God's rule in our own lives and multiply it in the lives of others by making disciples, through the power of the Holy Spirit, it seems reasonable to think of Christians fundamentally as kingdom builders.

[16]A. W. Tozer, *The Pursuit of God* (Harrisburg, PA: Christian Publications, 1982), 18.

hold as idols in our lives. Worse yet, we are often guilty of pursuing God solely because we think he offers the best option for obtaining those other things. Again, Tozer wrote:

> *The roots of our hearts have grown into things, and we dare not pull up one rootlet lest we die. Things have become necessary to us, a development never originally intended. God's gifts now take the place of God, and the whole course of nature is upset by the monstrous substitution.*[17]

Though, as professing Christians, we claim to be reborn into an otherworldly Savior, Jesus, our *God-and* lives can look eerily similar to the nonbeliever's next door. Consider, as one example among many, the decision about where to live. If someone were to offer us the chance to live anywhere in the world, in any neighborhood, and in any type of housing, then how would we go about choosing? What are the things we would look for in a location or a house? Which of those values is the *first* and most important? Which one trumps all the others? Again, what is our ultimate why?

If we are like most folks, professing Christians included, then our list would include considerations for some mix of the following: the type of neighborhood; crime statistics; school systems; parks and recreational opportunities; size of the house, garage, or yard; local nightlife; restaurant options; and proximity to work or church.

While there is nothing wrong with any of these considerations per se, the order in which we consider them matters a great deal. For instance, if we narrow down our potential locations by considering first the safety of a potential neighborhood or its proximity to a good school system, rather than how the location encourages us in godliness, then we may find, when we go to minister to others, that we have unwittingly placed ourselves far away from those who need us most. It is this order of priority that separates believers from unbelievers. As Jesus shared with a crowd long ago:

---

[17]Tozer, *Pursuit*, 22.

So do not worry, saying, "What shall we eat?" or "What shall we drink?" or "What shall we wear?" For the pagans run after all these things, and your heavenly Father knows that you need them. But seek first his kingdom and his righteousness, and all these things will be given to you as well.

—MATTHEW 6:31–33

The contrast is clear. Unbelieving pagans chase after the things of this world. Jesus's followers, on the other hand, seek God's kingdom first. Even the details most essential to earthly survival (what we eat, drink, and wear) are secondary to the preeminent pursuit of God's kingdom reign.

Jesus's words were spoken to a crowd full of ordinary people with ordinary lives, drawn to him by the good news he preached and by his power to transform lives both physically and spiritually. Their lives were full of important decisions and seemingly valid worries, just like ours. Jesus did not devalue earthly life or the physical body but urged the crowd to put their needs in proper context. "Seek first God's kingdom and his righteousness," Jesus told them, "and all these things will be given to you as well."[18]

Jesus's point is that when our priorities are clearly defined in order of importance, then our choices are much simpler; our time, talents, and treasure go to the first thing first, the second thing second, and so forth. However, when we try answering to multiple reference points of equal importance at the same time, our decisions become agonizing, confusing, and perhaps even damning.[19] As Jesus says a few verses earlier:

The eye is the lamp of the body. If your eyes are good {literally "single"}, your whole body will be full of light. But if your eyes are bad {by implication "multiple"}, your whole body will be full

---

[18]Matthew 6:33.
[19]Luke 16:13.

of darkness. If then the light within you is darkness, how great is that darkness!

No one can serve two masters. Either he will hate the one and love the other, or he will be devoted to the one and despise the other.

—MATTHEW 6:22–24

God's kingdom consists of those who submit wholly to his will of desire. To seek God's kingdom is to allow his rule (as evidenced by obedience) to expand in your own life and to encourage the same in the lives of those around you.

Jesus is not asking the crowd to stop eating or drinking. Rather, he is reminding them that the proper timing and mix of life's details depends on our preeminent kingdom reference point. No decision is benign. Even our decisions about what to drink and eat and wear are to be weighed according to how the different choices add or detract from the primary goal of God's kingdom expanding in us and in those we meet.

None of this is top-shelf or extra-credit Christianity. The singular and preeminent pursuit of God's rule is the lowest common denominator of our faith. It is the central command of Scripture, given many times in many ways from Genesis to Revelation. Yet the idea is so simple that most of us have probably never stopped to ask if we (or other professing Christians) have indeed committed ourselves to it unreservedly.

Do we know the one, true God, and are we truly pursuing his kingdom *first* in everything we think and do, with everything we have and are? The obvious answer is "No, of course not." For who could ever do that perfectly, this side of death or Jesus's second coming. Praise the Lord that he does not expect perfection, but gives us grace that is new every morning and sufficient to carry on to completion the work that he started in us.[20]

---

[20] Lamentations 3:22–23; Philippians 1:6.

Perhaps the better question for us is "Are we even *trying* to put God first?" While the pursuit will not be perfect, where the Spirit is (and he is in every true Christian), there will be at the very least a struggle for godliness and some evidence, however meager, of his fruit. If we are not making every effort, through his power, to put God's kingdom first in our hearts, minds, and lives, then the wonderful promise of Scripture is not ours and our lives are not only being wasted but are also earning us ever-increasing suffering in eternity. This is the hard lesson of the rich young ruler[21] and of other halfhearted followers of Christ.[22]

With our kingdom reference point in mind, let us consider again the decision about where to live that we explored previously. What if instead of seeking first the best school systems, safest neighborhoods, or the most pleasant geography, we looked for the place to live in which we would be most useful to God? Where we would we shine the most light? What location would limit our temptation to comfortable retreat and encourage us to bold witness and service? Are there places where the kingdom is undermanned and underarmed? What would it take to get us to such places?

The subtle and all-important step in any decision is the first one: deciding what we value most. Details are not forgotten, because the details affect our ability to yield to God's rule in our life and to spur on others to do the same.[23] But the details are not where we focus. Nor is one decision in life ever considered independent of the others, because our life, with all its interdependent pieces, only has one goal, which is to further God's kingdom reign.[24] To whatever degree we are able, we are expected to choose the particular bundle of details that seems to best cultivate godliness in ourselves and those around us.

---

[21] Matthew 19:16–30; Mark 10:17–31; Luke 18:18–30.

[22] Luke 9:57–62.

[23] The current details of our lives provide valuable clues regarding our reference points. For where our time, talents, and treasure are spent, there we will find our heart, as well.

[24] Matthew 6:31–33.

For the rest of this book, we will examine what would happen if we started with God and let our focus on him determine the details of our lives. While we often make this complicated, it is as simple as choosing our reference point and sticking with it. This is not an exhaustive study of theology or Christian living, but a primer for beginning the work of transferring the God-first theology of the Bible into a singular, balanced pursuit of him in everyday life.

The question that will be put to each of us repeatedly is this: What does it look like to use God's kingdom as my reference point in this situation rather than using the reference points of the world around me? While there are many examples given, these are ultimately irrelevant.

When it comes to the specifics, there is no one right way to live for God's glory in the Monday-through-Saturday grind of life. There is no one right place for all of us to live or one right career for all of us to have, and whether we get married or not, or to whom, will never be the real issue. Having the right motivation, or ultimate why, for whatever we do is what matters for eternity.

Colossians 3:1–17 serves as the template for our journey. While this passage is not unique, it does show, in elegant simplicity, the progression from kingdom-first thinking to kingdom-first living. We begin, in part one, with an exploration of Paul's exhortation to "set our minds on things above, not on earthly things."[25] The specific image we are to fix our minds and hearts on is that of Christ ruling in heaven "seated at the right hand of God."[26] To understand that image and its implications in our lives, we will start by tracing the progression of God's kingdom in history through the stages of creation, de-creation, and re-creation.

Parts two and three explore how the kingdom reference point necessarily leads us to "put to death whatever belongs to our earthly nature"[27] and to "put on the new self, which is being renewed in

---

[25] Colossians 3:2.

[26] Colossians 3:1.

[27] Colossians 3:5.

knowledge in the image of its Creator."[28] Using the kingdom-first lens, we will examine Paul's list of earthly practices, as well as his list of Christlike fruit. There will be many false reference points discussed along the way. The hope is not that we will pick ours off of any list and be done, but that we will learn (by way of examples) to use the kingdom-first lens to uncover our most entrenched idols, even those that do not appear in this book.

Finally, in part four, we will step back from the details to consider the more general exhortation "Whatever you do, whether in word or deed...do it all in the name of the Lord Jesus, giving thanks to God the Father through him."[29] The specific circumstances are left behind in hopes that we would not get lost in specific applications but learn to measure any and every decision according to its kingdom potential.

As our Creator, God has every right to demand whatever he wants of us, and demand he does, as we will see. Yet, as we consider those demands, we must constantly be reminding ourselves that the sacrifice pales in comparison to our very great reward. Otherwise, the cost will seem too high to our earthly selves, and we will continue to allow ourselves to be choked out by the worries of this world. See how Jesus describes our choice:

> *The kingdom of heaven is like treasure hidden in a field. When a man found it, he hid it again, and then in his joy went and sold all he had and bought that field.*
>
> *Again, the kingdom of heaven is like a merchant looking for fine pearls. When he found one of great value, he went away and sold everything he had and bought it.*
>
> —*MATTHEW 13:44–46*

---

[28] Colossians 3:10.

[29] Colossians 3:17.

We get beauty for ashes and joy in exchange for mourning.[30] All the stuff that we once clung to so tightly is seen as rubbish next to the all-surpassing wonder of being restored to our Creator and King—Father, Son, and Holy Spirit. He is *the* great reward of life, and when we see him as such, those things that looked like yokes, burdens, and sacrifices from outside his kingdom are transformed into opportunities for experiencing more of God's presence in our lives. When we choose to seize those opportunities, even the most mundane details of our lives will begin to bear witness to the worthiness of our King whose "loving kindness is better than life."[31]

---

[30] Isaiah 61:3.
[31] Psalm 63:3.

I
The King and His Kingdom

Since, then, you have been raised with Christ, set your hearts on things above, where Christ is seated at the right hand of God. Set your minds on things above, not on earthly things. For you died, and your life is now hidden with Christ in God. When Christ, who is your life, appears, then you also will appear with him in glory.

—COLOSSIANS 3:1–4

1

Creation (by God, for God)

Since, then, you have been raised with Christ, set your hearts on things above, where Christ is seated at the right hand of God. Set your minds on things above, not on earthly things.

—COLOSSIANS 3:1–2

Jesus Christ is King. He is reigning right now in heaven with God the Father. We who have died to the things of this world and submitted ourselves to Christ (i.e., true believers) have already been raised into that heavenly kingdom though we remain physically on earth. This is our spiritual reality, and it will be made plain for all to see when Jesus returns. For now, though, the reality is veiled and God's people are forced to pursue him by faith.[1]

Because our spiritual reality is veiled, it can be easy to get distracted. Earthly things, such as what we will eat, drink,

---

[1] Biblical faith is not unfounded fancy as many critics would make it out to be. Rather it is the certain hope—built on the goodness and sovereign power of God as evidenced throughout history—that he will indeed reward those who follow him (Hebrews 11:1).

and wear, will always scream at us for attention. This is why Scripture reminds us repeatedly to seek first the kingdom above, where Christ reigns. We are to set our hearts and minds on the King and let those details of our earthly life fall neatly in line with our new reality. For if we start with the details, distraction is inevitable.

The exhortation of Colossians 3:1-2 is not unique in Scripture.[2] The imagery of God alive, enthroned in heaven, is a dominant motif in the central narrative of Scripture. Whether it be through psalms, prophecies, the gospels, or apostolic letters, God's people are constantly reminded that God is "the blessed and only Ruler, the King of kings, and Lord of lords."[3] Thus, we have many places from which we could start our discussion of kingdom. For my part, though, I think it best to start at the beginning.

Before the beginning, there was nothing and nobody except God: no heavens, no earth, and no one to rule over. In those days, it made no sense to call God a king because, quite simply, he did not have a kingdom. That was all well and good, because God did not need a kingdom. He was content to be God, sharing his love among the three persons—Father, Son, and Holy Spirit—of the Godhead.

In the beginning, all of that changed. God created the heavens and the earth, and instantly, he had a kingdom, built by him and for him. He chose to establish his throne in the heavens, among the angels. From there, God ruled over all his works everywhere, including earth, which he refers to as his footstool.[4] God's exclusive claim to the throne is based on his exclusive role as Creator, as the praises of his people indicate:

---

[2] It is not even unique in the epistles. For example, a nearly identical call for singular focus on King Jesus can be found in Hebrews 12:2, which reads, "Let us fix our eyes on Jesus, the author and perfecter of our faith, who for the joy set before him endured the cross, scorning its shame, and sat down at the right hand of the throne of God."

[3] 1 Timothy 6:15.

[4] Psalm 103:19–22; Isaiah 66:1–2.

You are worthy, our Lord and God, to receive glory and honor and power, for you created all things, and by your will they were created and have their being.

—REVELATION 4:11

Scripture does not give us much, if any, insight into the creation of the heavens or angels. When it comes to the creation of the earth and humans, we do not get a whole lot more description.[5] Still, there are some important lessons to learn about God in the creation story.[6] Let us examine a few of those now.

Created Reality #1: God Alone Is King

In the beginning, God existed and nothing else. He is the lone, self-existent point from whom comes everything and everyone. If it exists, God made it—not from preassembled and pre-ordered ingredients, not even from scratch, but from nothing (*ex nihilo*). God's power is such that he did not even have to raise a hand to accomplish his creative designs. All God had to do was speak the words "Let there be..." and literally out of nowhere came the majestic heights of the Himalayas, the mysterious depths of the Pacific, and the incalculable expanses of the universe.

If you have ever stood at the foot of a mountain or at the edge of an ocean or simply looked up at the stars on a dark, clear night, then you have some sense of what God is like. It is in creation that God first reveals himself to humanity, giving visible evidence of "invisible

---

[5] Amazingly, despite all the attention we give the who and how of Earth's creation, only two of 1189 chapters in Scripture are devoted to this subject.

[6] In creation we learn of the character of our God, his purpose in creating us, and what relationships between God and humans, humans and humans, and humans and the rest of creation are to look like in a kingdom untainted by sin. As with all lists in this book, this one is not meant to be exhaustive. Rather, it is meant to highlight what is most essential to understanding God's kingdom and our role in it.

qualities—his eternal power and divine nature."[7] While we cannot know God fully by pondering his creation, it does give us an inkling of his complexity, beauty, order, and immeasurable strength.

The hero of the creation story, and every other story in Scripture, is God. We may argue over the details of how and when God created the heavens and the earth, but as true Christians, we cannot do away with God as Creator. Without that, we lose grounds for the humble worship of him and obedient submission to his purpose in creating us. As theologian J. I. Packer phrases it:

> *Knowing that God created the world around us, and ourselves as part of it, is basic to true religion. God is to be praised as Creator, by reason of the marvelous order, variety, and beauty of his works....Realizing our moment-by-moment dependence on God the Creator for our very existence makes it appropriate to live lives of devotion, commitment, gratitude, and loyalty toward him, and scandalous not to. Godliness starts here, with God the sovereign Creator as the first focus of our thoughts.*[8]

While the Genesis account of creation makes no explicit mention of Jesus, it is clear from the rest of Scripture that Jesus is God and was intimately involved in the creation of the heavens and earth.[9] Consider the opening lines to the gospel of John, for example, where Jesus is referred to figuratively as "the Word."

> *In the beginning was the Word, and the Word was with God, and the Word was God. He was with God in the beginning. Through him all things were made; without him nothing was made that has been made. In him was life, and that life was the light of men. The light shines in the darkness, but the darkness has not understood it.*

> —*JOHN 1:1–5*

---

[7] Romans 1:20.

[8] Packer, *Theology.*

[9] John 1:1–5.

Although Jesus was fully man and walked the earth, here Scripture claims that he was with God in the beginning. Not only was he with God, but Jesus also was (and is) God. The apostle Paul picks up on this theme of Jesus Christ's supremacy in creation during the opening chapter of Colossians:

For by him all things were created: things in heaven and on earth, visible and invisible, whether thrones or powers or rulers or authorities; all things were created by him and for him. He is before all things, and in him all things hold together.

—*COLOSSIANS 1:16–17*

As Creator, Jesus provides the natural datum, or solitary reference point, from which *everything* else derives its purpose and position. That is Paul's point in saying that all things were created by Jesus and for Jesus and are still held together in Jesus. He reigns supreme over all of his works, including us.

While every rock and tree and monkey points back to Christ in one way or another, none of creation is given the same honored position that we, as humans, are given in bearing Christ's image, or likeness. We get to portray the very character of God—compassionate, kind, humble, gentle, patient, forgiving, loving, and so forth—that Paul writes of in Colossians 3:12–13. We bear God's image to him, to each other, and to the rest of his creation.

Our image-bearing capacity is, of course, both an honor and a responsibility. When we bear God's image, we are submitting to his rule. That is how we obey him and fulfill our calling as humans. When we choose instead to bear the much-less-glorious image of the old self—immoral, greedy, angry, rageful, malicious, slanderous, and deceitful—which Paul writes of in Colossians 3:5, 8–9, then we have wandered away from God into sin and de-creation.[10]

---

[10] Colossians 3:5, 8–9.

Created Reality #2: Creation Exists to Worship God as King

Necessity may be the "mother of invention" for humans, but Scripture makes it clear that God did not create out of need.[11] Implied in his eternal self-existence is the characteristic of self-sufficiency. To put it in theological terms, the Triune God possesses aseity, which means that "He has life in himself and draws his unending energy from himself."[12] Paul explains God's aseity in the following terms:

The God who made the world and everything in it is the Lord of heaven and earth and does not live in temples built by hands. And he is not served by human hands, as if he needed anything, because he himself gives all men life and breath and everything else.

—ACTS 17:24–25

If God did not create out of need, then why? Simply put, God created a kingdom for himself so that he might be glorified and enjoyed as King. He desired worship, and so, for example, he created the heavens to declare his wonders, righteousness, and glory.[13] As David records:

Day after day they pour forth speech; night after night they display knowledge. There is no speech or language where their voice is not heard. Their voice goes out into all the earth, their words to the ends of the world.

—PSALM 19:2–4

Likewise, God created the earth, and everything in it, to worship him and bear witness to his glory. As another psalmist writes:

---

[11] Psalms 90:1–4; 102:25–27; Isaiah 40:28–31; John 5:26; Revelation 4:10.

[12] Packer, *Theology*.

[13] Psalm 50:6; Psalm 89:5; Psalm 97:6.

Sing to the Lord a new song; sing to the Lord, all the earth. Sing to the Lord, praise his name; proclaim his salvation day after day. Declare his glory among the nations, his marvelous deeds among all peoples.

—*PSALM 96:1–3*

At some level, all of creation points back to God as Creator and King. Yet, as we see in Genesis 1, humans are clearly set apart from the rest of earth's inhabitants, in both purpose and provision.

So God created man in his own image, in the image of God he created him; male and female he created them.

God blessed them and said to them, "Be fruitful and increase in number; fill the earth and subdue it. Rule over the fish of the sea and the birds of the air and over every living creature that moves on the ground."

—*GENESIS 1:27–28*

While animals were made according to their kind, God created men and women "in his own image." In other words, humans were given the unique ability to "make the real, Trinitarian God of the Bible... visible to the world."[14] Our distinction provides for both humility and dignity, reminding us that we are at all times below God and yet above the rest of creation. Driscoll and Breshears explain this notion of image bearing:

To image God is to "mirror" his invisible attributes to the world, somewhat like Moses, who radiated the glory of God after being in God's presence. Therefore, we are not to reflect Adam, the culture, or even ourselves to the world. Rather, God has bestowed upon us the amazing ability and awesome responsibility to be his mirrors

---

[14] Mark Driscoll and Gerry Breshears, *Doctrine* (Wheaton, IL: Crossway, 2010), 118.

on the earth, reflecting his goodness and glory to all for his glory and our joy. All persons are God's image in a basic sense, but Christians image him more than non-Christians, and mature Christians do even more so. [15]

The degree to which we fulfill our created purpose of mirroring God's invisible attributes to the world is directly related to our ability to set our hearts and minds on him. If we turn to the right or left, then we immediately begin mirroring something or someone else. In a world of distractions, such as ours, proper image bearing requires constant reorientation to Christ, our reference point. As Driscoll and Breshears go on to write:

Furthermore, image is both personal and communal. By personal, we mean that we as individual worshipers must continually ask ourselves whether we are good reflections of our God. By communal, we mean that churches, families, and other Christian communities must continually ask whether they are good reflections of God to one another and the world. [16]

In our self-assessment, it is absolutely crucial that we remember image bearing is not simply encompassed in what we *do*. Image bearing is who we *are* and thus encompasses every part of our body and mind. We must fight the urge to separate out any part of our living, breathing, thinking, feeling, moving, and doing as the means by which we image God to the world. Instead, we must make every effort to live a life of balanced godliness. Though we may be gifted, or given an extra measure of grace in certain areas, this does not mean we get to ignore those aspects of godliness that do not come as readily to us.

Moreover, image bearing is not a static activity. As image bearers, humans were created as stewards of God's kingdom. Our fundamental or default mission was to "fill the earth and subdue"[17]

---

[15] Driscoll and Breshears, *Doctrine*, 118–119.

[16] Driscoll and Breshears, *Doctrine*, 119.

[17] Genesis 1:28.

the world for God.[18] The prescribed means for accomplishing our mission was to "be fruitful and increase in number." Through multiplication of image bearers who were likewise under God's rule, we were not only to cover the surface of the earth with mirrors reflecting God's glory, but also with his kingdom reign. Though humans quickly disregarded this mandate, the principle remains.

Created Reality #3: Creation Exists to Enjoy God as King

God demands the worship of his creation and, at the same time, demands that we enjoy him. Indeed, as pastor and author John Piper has asserted, it seems that God is *most* glorified when we enjoy him. That is why psalm after psalm demands joy-filled worship, rather than emotionless and dutiful praise.[19] For example, take the opening verses of Psalm 47, written by the sons of Korah:

> *Clap your hands, all you nations; shout to God with cries of joy.*
> *How awesome is the Lord Most High, the great King over all the*
> *earth!*

> —*Psalm 47:1–2*

As Creator, the triune God is sovereign and answers to no one for his actions. He made everything and does with it exactly as he sees fit. This thought would be incredibly frightening except for the fact that God has forever bound his pleasure together with ours in creation. See how Piper explains the connection between our utmost joy and doing what pleases God:

---

[18] In subduing the world, it is important to understand that we are not bringing something that was outside of God's sovereign control under his control. For he has no need of man's help in exacting his will of decree upon our fellow humans or the rest of creation. Instead, by God's grace, we subdue the world in the sense that we are filling it, through his power, with those whose greatest delight is to do what pleases their King.

[19] Psalm 66:1–2.

We were made to experience full and lasting happiness from seeing and savoring the glory of God. If our best joy comes from something less, we are idolaters and God is dishonored. He created us in such a way that his glory is displayed through our joy in it. The gospel of Christ is the good news that at the cost of his Son's life, God has done everything necessary to enthrall us with what will make us eternally and ever-increasingly happy, namely, himself.

Long before Christ came, God revealed himself as the source of full and lasting pleasure. "You make known to me the path of life; in your presence there is fullness of joy; at your right hand are pleasures forevermore."[20] Then he sent Christ to suffer "that he might bring us to God." This means he sent Christ to bring us to the deepest, longest joy a human can have. Hear then the invitation: Turn from "the fleeting pleasures of sin"[21] and come to "pleasures forevermore." Come to Christ.[22]

Creation provides all the tangible evidence of God's incomprehensible power and love that we should ever need. This is particularly true for humans, who were not only uniquely purposed in creation, but also uniquely provided for. Rather than giving us an empty void to fill, God placed us in paradise with a toolbox full of tools. He created in abundance that we might not only live and spread his kingdom, but that we might do so with great joy and effectiveness.

Think for a moment of Adam and Eve's situation. They were placed in the middle of a verdant and plentiful garden, filled with trees that were "pleasing to the eye and good for food."[23] Everything they needed for the multiplication of image bearers, and much more, was theirs in abundance. Adam and Eve had each other, and what is more important, they enjoyed uninterrupted communion with God. The great reward of life was theirs.

---

[20] Psalm 16:11.

[21] Hebrews 11:25.

[22] John Piper, *For Your Joy* (Minneapolis, MN: Desiring God, 2009), 29–30.

[23] Genesis 2:9.

Even after the garden God's generosity and goodness were still evident. As Paul and Barnabas testified before the crowd at Lystra:

> *We are bringing you good news, telling you to turn from these worthless things to the living God, who made heaven and earth and sea and everything in them. In the past, he let all nations go their own way. Yet he has not left himself without testimony: He has shown kindness by giving you rain from heaven and crops in their seasons; he provides you with plenty of food and fills your hearts with joy.*
>
> —ACTS 14:15–17

Although creation was prepared both for our sustenance and our pleasure, we should not make the mistake of thinking that it is ours. We do not even belong to ourselves. God created us and sustains us. Every breath and thought and motivation toward him is a direct gift of God.[24] Likewise, creation has been lent to humans. We are to steward it in the way that best encourages God's rule in our own hearts and in the lives of those around us.[25]

Recap

All things were created by God and for God. He is the lone reference point from which everything else derives its purpose and position. As Creator, he rightly demands that he be worshiped and obeyed as the King of kings. Because God is loving and wants humans to experience the love of the Trinity, he also created us to find our greatest joy in close relationship with him. The beauty and abundance of creation serve as constant reminders of his love and tender concern for us.

---

[24] Psalm 104:29; John 15:16; Ephesians 2:8–9; Colossians 1:17.

[25] Encouraging God's rule, as we will see in chapters ten and eleven in particular, does not merely mean caring for the physical needs of those around us, but also for their spiritual needs as well. It is always both and never less.

As humans, we were created with the unique ability and responsibility of worshiping God through the bearing of his image. This is an honor unparalleled in creation and should inspire the kind of deep humility that David expresses in Psalm 8.

When I consider your heavens, the work of your fingers, the moon and the stars, which you have set in place, what is man that you are mindful of him, the son of man that you care for him? You made him a little lower than the heavenly beings and crowned him with glory and honor.

—*Psalm 8:3–5*

In our image bearing, there is no division between our "God" life and another secular life; all of it is to be lived *coram Deo*, or "before the face of God."[26] Thus, as we fix our eyes on the King, every aspect of our lives is to bear witness to the unique authority and worthiness of God. No thought or action or resource or relationship is off-limits when it comes to maximizing our ability to fill and subdue the earth through multiplication of image bearers.

---

[26] Driscoll and Breshears, *Doctrine*, 114.

2

De-Creation (The Revolt)

For although they knew God, they neither glorified him as God nor gave thanks to him, but their thinking became futile and their foolish hearts were darkened.

—ROMANS 1:21

It did not take long for humans to lose our reference point and stop thinking of our Creator God as the one true King. The rebellion began in heaven, with an angel named Satan leading the way. We are not told much about those circumstances. By the time we learn of Satan in Scripture, he has already left heaven and come to earth in hopes of enticing Adam and Eve, the first humans, to join his rival kingdom.

As we read the story of Adam and Eve's temptation and fall, we should keep in mind that God placed them in the middle of a garden of paradise. Their every need was provided for in abundance. They had a perfect relationship with God and each other. They had purpose and bore God's image faithfully and joyfully.

They also had food—more than they could ever need or want. As Scripture puts it:

The Lord God took the man and put him in the Garden of Eden to work it and take care of it. And the Lord God commanded the man, "You are free to eat from any tree in the garden; but you must not eat from the tree of the knowledge of good and evil, for when you eat of it you will surely die."

—*GENESIS 2:15–17*

Adam and Eve were not content to leave the fruit of the tree of the knowledge of good and evil alone. Even in a garden lovingly crafted for them, Satan was able to tempt them to look away from God long enough to plant a seed of doubt in their minds. Satan, taking the form of a serpent, approached Eve, first questioning God's command and then boldly accusing God of lying to keep Adam and Eve from becoming gods themselves.

"You will not surely die," the serpent said to the woman. "For God knows that when you eat of it your eyes will be opened, and you will be like God, knowing good and evil."

—*GENESIS 3:4–5*

Adam and Eve let this doubt in the goodness of God's sovereignty give way to discontentment and disobedience. They ought to have gratefully enjoyed the garden full of trees that were "pleasing to the eye and good for food,"[27] but instead, they chose to focus on the one thing denied them. Rather than seeing God's loving hand protecting them from death, they chose to believe the worst about him and his motives.

The decision to eat from the tree of the knowledge of good and evil seems innocuous enough, but the results were devastating. The

---

[27] Genesis 2:9.

course of God's kingdom presence on earth was changed forever. When Adam and Eve chose to not obey God, they were rejecting his will of desire and, thus his rule and kingship in their lives. They were following Satan's lead in establishing a kingdom for themselves, and their sinful rebellion caused an unraveling of the natural, created order.

Every human since Adam and Eve has been born into this state of de-creation and, more specifically, the rival kingdom that has set itself up against the one true King. When Jesus Christ came into the world, he ushered in the beginnings of a return of the kingdom of heaven to earth that continues to grow even today. Yet our world remains in bondage to decay and will continue to do so until he returns again to make all things new. Before we can answer our call to seek first the kingdom, we must acknowledge a few of the realities of our de-created state.

De-Created Reality #1: Everyone Sins

Beginning with Adam's disobedience, sinful rebellion became humanity's new nature, or default mode of operation, in the world. As it is written, "Sin entered the world through one man, and death through sin, and in this way death came to all men, because all sinned."[28] In some form or another, humans inherit from our first parents a disposition toward unfaithfulness. Living under God's rule as image bearers is not what seems most natural anymore. Rather, we are born with a partiality to earthly reference points and a baseline disregard for God's desires.

If we follow the story of humanity beyond Genesis 3, where the first sin is recorded, we can see just how quickly sin became the norm for our ancestors. In the very next chapter, for example, the first murder occurs, and only two chapters after that we find one of the most sobering assessments of humanity's universal depravity ever written.

---

[28] Romans 5:12.

The Lord saw how great man's wickedness on the earth had become, and that every inclination of the thoughts of his heart was only evil all the time. The Lord was grieved that he had made man on the earth, and his heart was filled with pain. So the Lord said, "I will wipe mankind, whom I have created, from the face of the earth—men and animals, and creatures that move along the ground, and birds of the air—for I am grieved that I have made them."

—Genesis 6:5–7

Shortly after these verses, Scripture records that the Lord did indeed send a flood to wipe mankind (except for Noah and his family) from the face of the earth. There was nothing exceptional about the wickedness of the people in the world at that time. In fact, it was downright ordinary in comparison to modern times. As Jesus later informs us, the people of Noah's day were simply going about life as usual: "eating and drinking, marrying and giving in marriage, up to the day Noah entered the ark."[29]

Stories like this are shocking. It is hard to imagine our good and loving God drowning all these men, women, and children. Were they really that bad? Are we really that bad? The answer for both groups is, of course, yes! But to understand that answer, we must learn to see life from God's perspective, not our own. We are not the innocent and misguided wanderers we like to think we are; neither were the folks in Noah's day (Noah and his family included).

God looks at humanity's de-created mode of operation and sees that *every* inclination of the thoughts of our hearts is *only* evil *all* the time. Instead of fixing our hearts and minds on our King, reflecting his unique authority and worth, we are God's enemies—evil by nature and by choice. We are born into a rebel kingdom and daily choose to take up arms against our rightful King. Scripture

---

[29] Matthew 24:38.

describes us as "alienated and hostile in mind" toward God.[30] There is no innocence about us.

If we are to have any hope of redemption, we must put away all notions of being good people. Next to God's holy otherness, our best deeds are nothing more than filthy rags. If we are to imagine ourselves on some cosmic scale that weighs our good deeds on one side and our bad ones on the other, we must realize that we are only capable of adding to the side weighing the bad deeds. See how Paul summarizes Scripture's teaching on man's goodness:

> *There is no one righteous, not even one; there is no one who understands, no one who seeks God. All have turned away, they have together become worthless; there is no one who does good, not even one. Their throats are open graves; their tongues practice deceit. The poison of vipers is on their lips. Their mouths are full of cursing and bitterness. Their feet are swift to shed blood; ruin and misery mark their ways, and the way of peace they do not know. There is no fear of God before their eyes.*

—*ROMANS 3:10–18*

De-Created Reality #2: Everyone Deserves Death

Most often we think of death in one dimension, as the moment our bodies give way, when the last breath is drawn and the last beat of the heart is sounded. This is the form of death most readily obvious in our lives and in stories like the flood where we see God actively judging sin. It looms imminently and ominously ahead, reminding us of our mortality and our finiteness.

However, we can see from the example of Adam and Eve that death has both physical and spiritual dimensions. On the physical level, their bodies did eventually give way, but first they experienced the spiritual death of separation from God. Left unchecked,

---

[30] Colossians 1:21.

this separation will continue on for eternity in the lake of fire, in what Scripture refers to as the second death.[31] [32]

As Adam and Eve demonstrate, we experience the firstfruits of this spiritual death while we are still physically alive on earth. Adam and Eve began life in face-to-face communion with God. They were sinless, with nothing to hide. With sin, however, everything changed. Immediately after eating the forbidden fruit, and without any direction from God, Adam and Eve experienced guilt and shame, which drove them to cover their nakedness and hide from God.[33] Instinctively, they felt a need for separation between sinful man and holy God that was confirmed when God cast them out of the Garden of Eden.

In kingdom language, Scripture describes humanity's de-created and separated position as participation in the "domain of darkness."[34] In sharp and purposeful contrast, we read that "God is light; in him there is no darkness at all."[35] God cannot abide with sin simply because it is not who he is.[36] By nature, he is set apart as other from the sinful norm of humankind. It is this *otherness* that Scripture refers to as godliness or holiness.

Separation from God is not a static reality but a progressive one. As long as we persist in sin, unregenerated by the Holy Spirit, we wander further and further from God, adopting one ungodly value on top of another. With our hearts and minds no longer anchored on God, we are "tossed back and forth by the waves, and blown here and there by every wind of teaching and by the cunning and crafti-

---

[31] Revelation 2:10; 20:13–15.

[32] We may be tempted to minimize or do away with eternal suffering to make God sound more loving, but God's Word does not bend so easily. It remains emphatic that sinful man, along with Satan and all the fallen angels, will justly suffer forever in the lake of fire as traitors against a good and loving Creator. We do ourselves, and those around us, no favors when we ignore this reality that Jesus took great care to warn us about (Matthew 5:22, 29–30; 10:28; 18:9; 25:30, 41).

[33] Genesis 3:6–8.

[34] Colossians 1:13.

[35] 1 John 1:5.

[36] Galatians 5:16–17.

ness of men in their deceitful scheming."[37] See how Paul described humanity's wandering in his letter to the Romans:

> *For although they knew God, they neither glorified him as God nor gave thanks to him, but their thinking became futile and their foolish hearts were darkened. Although they claimed to be wise, they became fools and exchanged the glory of the immortal God for images made to look like mortal man and birds and animals and reptiles.*
>
> *Therefore God gave them over in the sinful desires of their hearts to sexual impurity for the degrading of their bodies with one another. They exchanged the truth of God for a lie, and worshiped and served created things rather than the Creator—who is forever praised. Amen.*
>
> —ROMANS 1:21–25

Humans never stop worshiping. That is to say, it is impossible for us to be truly godless. If we stop giving honor and attention to one object of worship, then we have merely moved on and replaced our first object of worship with another that we find more appealing.

Still, it is easy to distance ourselves from the folks Paul describes in the passage above. Few professing Christians these days are likely to be found bowing down to "images made to look like mortal man and birds and animals and reptiles." Yet we should not be so quick to assume that we are worshiping God and not simply claiming his name.

So often our priorities and values tell a different story than our lips, which so readily say, "Lord, Lord" to Jesus.[38] If we take a sober look at our priorities, both spoken and unspoken, many of us will find that we are indeed willing idolaters, worshiping and serving

---

[37] Ephesians 4:14.

[38] Matthew 7:21–23.

"created things rather than the Creator." For, at its root, an idol is *anything* other than God that commands the attention of our heart, mind, soul, or strength, to such a degree that it competes with God for the first and best of our time, energy, talents, and resources.[39]

De-Created Reality #3: Everyone Is Hopelessly Lost

As wanderers go, we are thoroughly lost. Our problem is that our reference points are all messed up, and left to ourselves, we do not even care to set them straight. Godlessness and idolatry are now as natural and ubiquitous to us as the air we breathe. They underlie our assumptions and guide our decisions, giving us eyes that do not see and ears that do not hear.[40] We do not know the way back to God, nor do we care to.[41]

Just as a leopard cannot change its spots, we cannot turn our rebellious hearts toward God[42] or make what is unclean, clean again.[43] Our attempts at morality have "an appearance of wisdom, with their self-imposed worship, their false humility, and their harsh treatment of the body, but they lack any value in restraining sensual indulgence."[44] Thus, Scripture reminds us that we are *dead* (not struggling) in our sin and could no more help ourselves than a drowned corpse could grab hold of a lifeline.[45]

At this point, we may wonder, "Are we not making choices all the time, including whether to follow God?" This question brings us back to the distinction between free agency and free will. For

---

[39] Whether your focus is on family, career, sex, education, money, cars, fame, health, houses, mission, sacrifice, community, or justice, it does not matter. It is God first and alone, or it is idolatry. I write this not to discourage you with your current state of affairs, but to spur you on toward the one true treasure.

[40] Jeremiah 5:21.

[41] Romans 8:7–8; 1 Corinthians 2:14.

[42] Jeremiah 13:23.

[43] Job 14:4.

[44] Colossians 2:23.

[45] Ephesians 2:1, 5.

insight into this distinction, I defer again to theologian J. I. Packer, who writes:

Free agency is a mark of human beings as such. All humans are free agents in the sense that they make their own decisions as to what they will do, choosing as they please in the light of their sense of right and wrong and the inclinations they feel. Thus they are moral agents, answerable to God and each other for their voluntary choices. So was Adam, both before and after he sinned; so are we now, and so are the glorified saints who are confirmed in grace in such a sense that they no longer have it in them to sin. Inability to sin will be one of the delights and glories of heaven, but it will not terminate anyone's humanness; glorified saints will still make choices in accordance with their nature, and those choices will not be any the less the product of human free agency just because they will always be good and right.

Free will, however, has been defined by Christian teachers from the second century on as the ability to choose all the moral options that a situation offers, and Augustine affirmed against Pelagius and most of the Greek Fathers that original sin has robbed us of free will in this sense. We have no natural ability to discern and choose God's way because we have no natural inclination Godward; our hearts are in bondage to sin, and only the grace of regeneration can free us from that slavery. This, for substance, was what Paul taught in Romans 6:16–23; only the freed will (Paul says, the freed person) freely and heartily chooses righteousness. A permanent love of righteousness—that is, an inclination of heart to the way of living that pleases God—is one aspect of the freedom that Christ gives (John 8:34–36; Galatians 5:1, 13).[46]

That is, in short, the difference between free agency and free will. Much more can be said, and has, about the relationship between our free agency and God's sovereignty. It seems that these truths are

---

[46] *Concise Theology.*

held somewhat like bookends in Scripture, to keep us wandering too far toward either licentiousness, in the case of free agency with its emphasis on man's responsibility, or toward legalism, in the case of God's sovereignty with its emphasis on man's depravity and God's sure-handed grace. Where the two come together, there is the grace-motivated godliness of the true disciple.

Recap

The state of affairs in our fallen and broken world is this: God is good, and we are not. He is the all-powerful, all-good Creator, and we are his traitorous creation. In de-creation, mankind's image-bearing capacity was not lost so much as misdirected. As fallen humans, we no longer submit to God's will of desire, preferring instead to sit on the throne of our lives. Like Adam, we are too busy questioning God's love and God's authority to obey him. The result is that we use creation, including other humans, in ways that build our own kingdoms and maximize our affluence, comfort, and security rather than God's loving rule.

Yet despite all our efforts to get away from God, we are still rulers under a ruler. Scripture describes our fallen world as the "domain of darkness" where Satan reigns.[47] He is the "god of this age" who blinds "the minds of unbelievers, so that they cannot see the light of the gospel of the glory of Christ."[48] His goal is to thwart God's rule in our lives by distracting us from our single-minded pursuit of God's kingdom.[49]

While God allows humans to pursue the desires of their "darkened hearts" and "depraved minds,"[50] he still reigns sovereignly over everything, including Satan.[51] God is not content to simply enforce his sovereign will on humans, though; he rightly and

---

[47] Colossians 1:13; 1 John 5:19.

[48] 2 Corinthians 4:4.

[49] 2 Corinthians 11:3–4.

[50] Romans 1:21, 28.

[51] Psalm 47:2, 7; 1 John 4:4.

jealousy desires to be our greatest treasure, the one worth selling or casting aside everything else, with joy, to obtain. God also desires to be King on earth, just as he is in heaven, where submission to his will of desire (not just his sovereign will) is still the default mode of operation.

In our pride, we will be tempted to live life on our own terms, and we will continue to settle for the false reference points of lesser gods. Praise the Lord, however, that in his great mercy, he will frustrate every move of his people so long as we seek rest in anything other than our Creator. He does so in the hope that we would be "liberated from [our] bondage to decay and brought into the glorious freedom of the children of God."[52] Frustration cuts through our darkened hearts in ways that peace and affluence do not. It forces us to yearn for something more—a way out, or back, to our King.

---

[52] Romans 8:21.

3

Re-Creation (The King Returns)

But you, Bethlehem Ephrathah, though you are small among the clans of Judah, out of you will come for me one who will be ruler over Israel, whose origins are from of old, from ancient times.

— MICAH 5:2

Only the first two chapters of Scripture are devoted to the story of earth's creation. The third chapter records humanity's fall and the beginning of de-creation. With those elements in place, the rest of Scripture (1186 chapters) is spent telling "the long story of 'redemption,' how God rescues his people from the enemy's clutches, restores them back into his image, and (finally) will re-create them 'in a new heaven and new earth.'"[53]

Our first inkling of God's plan for re-creation and redemption comes even as he is dealing out judgment for humanity's first sin. Death would not always reign, he promised, because one day a

---

[53] Gordon D. Fee and Douglas Stuart, *How to Read the Bible for All Its Worth* (Grand Rapids, MI: Zondervan, 2003), 90.

child would be born from Adam and Eve's descendants, who would rise to crush the head of the great tempter, Satan.[54] By crushing Satan, this child would defeat death forever so that one day God's people could say with confidence "Where, O death, is your victory? Where, O death, is your sting?"[55]

For many years the world waited, slowly crumbling under the weight of its sin. While God continued to accomplish his sovereign purposes without fail, he still desired to have people on earth who would fix their hearts and minds on him, delighting to serve and worship him as King. So he raised up a kingdom for himself out of sinful humanity, starting with a man named Abram (who was eventually renamed Abraham). See how the Lord describes his purpose in calling Abraham:

> *Abraham will surely become a great and powerful nation, and all nations on earth will be blessed through him. For I have chosen him, so that he will direct his children and his household after him to keep the way of the Lord by doing what is right and just.*

> —GENESIS 18:18–19

From Abraham's descendants God brought forth the nation Israel, which was to be to God and to the world around it "a kingdom of priests."[56] It was never enough among God's people to say that he existed or that he created the world. To be his subject meant to submit wholly and unreservedly to his rule and to lead others into the same worshipful obedience of the one true God. We can see this idea again in the summary address given to the Israelites before they took possession of the Promised Land:

---

[54] Genesis 3:15.

[55] 1 Corinthians 15:55.

[56] Exodus 19:6.

Hear, O Israel: The Lord our God, the Lord is one. Love the Lord your God with all your heart and with all your soul and with all your strength. These commandments that I give you today are to be upon your hearts. Impress them on your children. Talk about them when you sit at home and when you walk along the road, when you lie down and when you get up. Tie them as symbols on your hands and bind them on your foreheads. Write them on the doorframes of your houses and on your gates.

—DEUTERONOMY 6:4–9

In both the passage from Genesis and in the one from Deuteronomy, we see a repetition of humanity's created calling to spread God's preeminent rule through the multiplication of image bearers who are focused on the true King. The difference is that now the command is being given to sinful people in a sinful world. Rather than just procreating their way to healthy image bearers, now God's people were (and are) to multiply his rule in human hearts through intentional invitation and instruction.

As each one loved God with his whole heart, his whole soul, and the whole of his strength, the Israelites were meant to shine forth to the nations the otherworldly character of God, inviting all into worshipful service of the true King. But instead of using God as their reference point, everyone did what was right in his own eyes.[57] Israel rejected God as King and followed after all manner of idols and human kings.[58] The result was that they began to mirror the fallen, selfish, and oppressive nature of the nations around them.

God was still gracious and provided for Israel through human kings, like David, who enjoyed great military and political success. Eventually, though, the Israelites' sinful wandering progressed to the point that they became indistinguishable from the nations

---

[57] Judges 21:25.

[58] 1 Samuel 8:7.

around them. Consequently, God allowed them to be overtaken by their enemies and scattered.

Despite all of this, God did not give up on his people. In exile he continued to remind them, as he had in the fall, that one day things would be different—that a different kind of King would reign over God's people.[59] He sent prophet after prophet with a message of the promise of restoration and re-creation. Unlike with David, there would be no end to the new King's government. His throne would last forever[60] and stretch to the "ends of the earth."[61]

Finally, after years of waiting, the appointed time arrived and God made good on all of his promises by sending his only begotten Son, Jesus Christ, to rescue his people. As triumphant arrivals go, Jesus's was somewhat unorthodox. The great King was born to a virgin in a stable in the town of Bethlehem. His birth was announced only to a few shepherds who came and worshiped him.

Eight days later, a prophet and prophetess at the temple welcomed the King's arrival.[62] Jesus's family returned to Bethlehem where, some time later, a star led a group of learned astronomers from the East to their doorstep. These men also worshipped him as the King of the Jews. When Herod, who was king of Israel at that time, found out about Jesus, he feared for his throne and had all the boys less than two years old in Bethlehem killed. Jesus escaped with his family to Egypt after God warned Joseph, Mary's husband, in a dream of the coming danger.[63]

After the danger had passed, Jesus and his parents moved to Nazareth, where they settled down to live. We do not know much about this time in Nazareth, only that during it, "Jesus grew in wisdom and stature, and in favor with God and men."[64] When

---

[59] Psalm 2:1–12; Psalm 10:16–18.

[60] Isaiah 9:7.

[61] Zechariah 9:10.

[62] Luke 2:1–38.

[63] Matthew 2:1–23.

[64] Luke 2:52.

Jesus was roughly thirty years old, he left Nazareth to begin his public ministry.

This ministry began with an announcement: "Repent, for the kingdom of God is at hand."[65] He followed up the announcement by going from town to town preaching the good news of the kingdom.[66] Jesus had great compassion for the physical and spiritual depravity around him, healing many and offering forgiveness for sins. However, he did not shy away from calling out sin and idolatry when he saw it, or from demanding repentance. Everything Jesus did, he did as one with authority, on the basis of a number of absolute and exclusive claims.

Jesus claimed to be *the* source of true life apart from which we are fit for nothing.[67] He claimed to be *the* light that allows us to see in a world darkened by sin.[68] Moreover, he claimed to be *the* way to enter into salvation, which is that eternal rest that all religions seek, but only his followers find.[69] He claimed to be the Ruler of an otherworldly kingdom.[70] In short, Jesus claimed to be the one true God, returning to restore his de-created people.[71]

However, this kingdom was something altogether different from what the Jews expected.[72] Years of oppression had made them long for a king like David, who would throw off Israel's enemies. Yet God did not want a refurbished earthly kingdom with geographic boundaries and military might. Instead, God wanted to bring his heavenly kingdom to earth.[73] He wanted to rejoin his people as their King[74] and rule in their hearts the way he rules in

---

[65] Matthew 4:17 (ESV).

[66] Matthew 4:23–25.

[67] John 6:35, 53; 15:1, 5.

[68] John 8:12; 9:5.

[69] John 10:7, 9; 11:25; 14:6.

[70] John 18:36.

[71] Matt 26:63–66; 27:39–43; John 5:18.

[72] Isaiah 43:19.

[73] Zechariah 14:9.

[74] Isaiah 7:14; Matthew 1:22.

the hearts of the angelic beings who serve him day and night in heaven.[75] As Jesus taught his disciples:

The kingdom of God does not come with your careful observation, nor will people say, "Here it is," or "There it is," because the kingdom of God is within you.

—LUKE 17:20–21

And, again, in a lesson on prayer:

This, then, is how you should pray: "Our Father in heaven, hallowed be your name, your kingdom come, your will be done on earth as it is in heaven."

—MATTHEW 6:9–10

The parallel and synonymous connection Jesus makes in this second passage between the Father's kingdom coming and his will being done "on earth as it is in heaven" is unmistakable. When combined with the first passage, it becomes clear that the kingdom of God exists in hearts that are obedient to his will of desire. While we will not walk through all the passages in Scripture that mention the kingdom of God, many scholars affirm the fundamental truth behind the two above.

Biblical scholar George Eldon Ladd, for example, summarizes his understanding of the kingdom of God in the following terms:

The Kingdom of God is the redemptive reign of God dynamically active to establish his rule among human beings, and that this Kingdom, which will appear as an apocalyptic act at the end of the age, has already come into human history in the person and

---

[75] Isaiah 59:20; Matthew 1:21.

mission of Jesus to overcome evil, to deliver people from its power, and to bring them into the blessings of God's reign.[76]

J. I. Packer similarly writes:

The theme of the kingdom of God runs through both Testaments, focusing God's purpose for world history. In Old Testament times God declared that he would exercise his kingship (his sovereignty, Daniel 4:34–35) by setting up his kingdom (his rule or reign over people's lives and circumstances) under his chosen king (the Davidic Messiah, Isaiah 9:6–7) in a golden age of blessing. This kingdom came with Jesus the Messiah as a worldwide relational reality, existing wherever the lordship of Jesus is acknowledged in repentance, faith, and new obedience. Jesus, the Spirit-anointed, Spirit-filled ruler-designate (Luke 3:21–22; 4:1, 14, 18–21, 32–36, 41), died, rose, ascended, and is now enthroned in heaven as ruler over all things (Matthew 28:18; Colossians 1:13), King of kings and Lord of lords (Revelation 17:14; 19:16).[77]

And Driscoll and Breshears explain it this way:

At its simplest, the kingdom of God is the result of God's mission to rescue and renew his sin-marred creation. The kingdom of God is about Jesus our king establishing his rule and reign over all creation, defeating the human and angelic evil powers, bringing order to all, enacting justice, and being worshiped as Lord.[78]

As each of these synopses makes clear, the defining characteristic of God's kingdom is obedient submission to his will of desire. Jesus brought this heavenly kingdom into human history. As God, he

---

[76] Kevin DeYoung and Ted Kluck, *Why We're Not Emergent* (Chicago, IL: Moody, 2008), 185 (quoting George Eldon Ladd, *A Theology of the New Testament,* rev. ed. [Grand Rapids: Erdman's, 1993], 68ff.).

[77] *Concise Theology.*

[78] *Doctrine,* 411.

demanded the singular obedience of his followers (and he continues to demand the same of believers in our day). Unlike the earthly kingdom of Israel, no halfhearted subjects were allowed in the kingdom of heaven.[79]

Wholeheartedness does not equal perfection. For while the spirit of God within us is happy to think, say, and do the things of God, our earthly nature will fight to the death against our sanctification.[80] We see this reality on display in the lives of the disciples, who had given everything up to follow Jesus but still stumbled from time to time.[81]

The difference between an unbeliever and a believer, or a traitor and a subject of the King, is not presence (or lack) of sin. Rather, it is the joyful willingness of the true believer, when confronted with a previously unknown idol, to humbly repent, eagerly throw off that distraction, and fix his gaze once more on Jesus, the Author and Perfecter of his faith.[82] This preeminent desire for God, while a constant struggle on earth, is nonnegotiable for entrance into the kingdom of heaven, and it is found only in those whose hearts have been made alive—from stone to flesh—by the Holy Spirit.[83]

While huge crowds gathered to be fed by Jesus's miracles, few could stomach his exclusive call on their lives. They wanted the peripheral blessings of the kingdom but not the King himself. It seems that those in worldly positions of power and authority felt particularly threatened by Jesus's authoritative claim to mankind's obedience, and so they had him—the God-man and only human to ever live a sinless life—crucified on a cross.[84] His lifeless body was

---

[79] Luke 9:57–62; Matthew 19:13–26; Mark 10:17–27; Luke 18:18–23.

[80] Romans 7:21–25; Galatians 5:17.

[81] Consider the apostle Peter, for example, who denied Christ before his death (John 18:15–18, 25–27) and was restored after it to become the leader of the early church (John 21:15–19). Even after being given the Holy Spirit at Pentecost, Peter was still susceptible to sin, as we see him being led astray by the "circumcision group" before being corrected by Paul (Galatians 2:11–21).

[82] Hebrews 12:1–2.

[83] Ezekiel 36:26; John 3:3–6, 14–15.

[84] John 11:47–53.

laid in a tomb with a giant stone covering the entrance and Roman soldiers to guard it.

Ironically, it was in this ultimate act of rebellion with creation killing Creator that the gate to the kingdom of heaven was finally reopened to humans. As fallen creatures we could not simply ask for forgiveness and walk back into relationship with God. Someone still had to die to pay for our sin, and that someone was Jesus. As Creator, he had every right to destroy his rebellious creation once and for all. However, God bore with us in great love and mercy, choosing to humble himself and suffer at the hands of his ungrateful creation.

You see, at just the right time, when we were still powerless, Christ died for the ungodly. Very rarely will anyone die for a righteous man, though for a good man someone might possibly dare to die. But God demonstrates his own love for us in this: While we were still sinners, Christ died for us.

Since we have now been justified by his blood, how much more shall we be saved from God's wrath through him! For if, when we were God's enemies, we were reconciled to him through the death of his Son, how much more, having been reconciled, shall we be saved through his life!

—*ROMANS 5:6–10*

Jesus did indeed come back to life. On the third day after his death, Jesus's tomb was found inexplicably empty. While the disciples waited fearfully in secret, neither the Romans nor the Jewish leaders could produce a body. Then Jesus appeared, not as a phantom, but as one you could physically touch and who ate real food.[85] He appeared to over five hundred people before leaving the disciples to rejoin God the Father in heaven.[86] Many of these people later

---

[85] Luke 24:36–48.

[86] 1 Corinthians 15:6.

lost their lives for testifying to the resurrection and deity of Jesus Christ. Author Lee Strobel points out the unique nature of the first disciples' testimonies:

> *While most people can only have faith that their beliefs are true, the disciples were in a position to know without a doubt whether or not Jesus had risen from the dead. They claimed that they saw him, talked with him, and ate with him. If they weren't absolutely certain, they wouldn't have allowed themselves to be tortured to death for proclaiming the Resurrection had happened.*[87]

Before Jesus left, he laid out one last time for his disciples what it meant to seek first his kingdom on earth. Now, given that Jesus's kingdom is the same kingdom that we have been following from the beginning—the one that exists only in the hearts of God's wholly devoted disciples—his parting words should not surprise us.

> *Then Jesus came to them and said, "All authority in heaven and on earth has been given to me. Therefore go and make disciples of all nations, baptizing them in the name of the Father and of the Son and of the Holy Spirit, and teaching them to obey everything I have commanded you. And surely I am with you always, to the very end of the age."*

> —*MATTHEW 28:18–20*

Although this passage has often been referred to as *The* Great Commission, it is hardly unique in the gospels, let alone Scripture.[88] The command to make disciples is simply a restating of Israel's mandate to observe and pass on singular love for God, which, as we have seen already, is itself a restatement of the creation mandate to

---

[87] Lee Strobel, *The Case for Christ* (Grand Rapids, MI: Zondervan, 1998), 334.

[88] Mark 16:15–16; John 20:21; Acts 1:7–8. The variation between the accounts likely indicates that Jesus thought the command was important enough to be repeated on multiple occasions.

fill and subdue the earth through multiplication of image bearers. As J. I. Packer writes:

> *The task of the church is to make the invisible kingdom visible through faithful Christian living and witness-bearing. The gospel of Christ is still the gospel of the kingdom (Matthew 4:23; 24:14; Acts 20:25; 28:23, 31), the good news of righteousness, peace, and joy in the Holy Spirit through entering a disciple's relationship to the living Lord (Romans 14:17). The church must make its message credible by manifesting the reality of kingdom life.*[89]

Two thousand years later, our call is the same. We are to fix our eyes singularly on the King, that we might be filled with his light and pass it along to others still stumbling about in darkness.[90] We are, like Israel of old, to be a kingdom of priests who seek to restore, through word and deed, our fellow sinners to their Creator and Lord.[91]

The process of restoration is the process of making disciples. It begins with us becoming disciples who learn what it means to measure our every thought, word, and deed by the reference point of God's kingdom, rather than the broken reference points of our world. Only as the Spirit of God focuses our appetite on those things that add to the kingdom are we able to cultivate a singular love in others.

Though parts of this book deal directly with *making* disciples of others, the majority of the book is intentionally spent exploring what it means to *become* disciples of Jesus ourselves.[92] This is not to make less of our command to pass on our singular love of God to

---

[89] *Concise Theology*.

[90] Matthew 5:14–16.

[91] 2 Corinthians 5:17–21; Revelation 1:6.

[92] Jesus's notion of discipleship was (and is) much more robust than our current notions of mentor-mentee relationships or book club–like small groups. Making disciples, as Jesus describes it in Matthew 28:18–20, involves everything that can be thought of as ministry: seeking out spiritual and physical need, initiating unbelievers into God's fold, and training up believers to obey everything Jesus commanded. See Appendix 4.

others, for that is inseparable from God-first living. Rather, it is to keep us from making the devastating yet all-too-common mistake of trying to make disciples before we have begun to experience that transformation ourselves.

4

The Re-Created Life
(Default Christianity)

You have taken off your old self with its practices and have put on the new self, which is being renewed in knowledge in the image of its Creator.

—*COLOSSIANS 3:9–10*

Left to ourselves, our condition is very bleak, but the image of Jesus alive and sitting on the throne gives us great hope. It emphasizes the victorious reign of our Lord, who did for us what we could never do for ourselves. He is the promised Savior who defeated death and Satan at the cross, by paying the price for our sins and offered us the hope of new life by being resurrected from the dead. Hope in Jesus is the best kind of hope, because it does not disappoint.

When Jesus re-creates us, he marks us "in him with a seal, the promised Holy Spirit, who is a deposit guaranteeing our inheritance until the redemption of those who are God's possession—to the praise of his glory."[93] With the Holy Spirit inside of us, bearing God's image accurately is not only possible; it is inevitable. For just as good trees bear good fruit, so God trees bear God fruit.

God's sovereignty is meant to encourage us in our bumbling brokenness. However, it does not do away with our responsibility to respond. For even while we are assured that the Holy Spirit lives in us and is carrying on to certain completion the work of salvation that he started in us,[94] Scriptures' commands are still pointed at us, calling us to take an active role in making manifest our hidden shift in realities.

There is an eternal difference between knowing about Jesus Christ and giving him (and his kingdom) first importance in our lives. Simply acknowledging the facts of Jesus's life or even his sovereignty is not enough, for even hell-bound demons know that Jesus exists and that he is the Son of God.[95] To be saved and enjoy him for eternity, we must submit ourselves wholeheartedly and unreservedly to his purpose as King of kings.

But what does re-created life, or default-mode Christianity, look like and sound like? What is the proper response to God's loving grace? What are the works that believers bear in keeping with their repentance, and what does giving God top priority mean, not just in prayers or songs or service trips, but in our choice of jobs, locations, hobbies, and local churches? Should each of us sell everything we have and give the money to a church or to the poor? Are you and I called to cross-cultural missions or to end human trafficking, or is that somebody else's job?

While we may be tempted to lose ourselves in these kinds of details, the proper response is quite simple. Using the kingdom of God as our solitary reference point leads us to "take off [our] old self with its practices, and…[to] put on the new self, which is being renewed in knowledge in the image of its Creator."[96] We follow Christ's lead, passing through death to life, pure and full of joy as

---

[93] Ephesians 1:13–14.

[94] Philippians 1:6.

[95] Matthew 8:28.

[96] Colossians 3:10.

was intended in creation. This new life is wholly in Christ, with every piece chosen for its ability to further his glory.

Simple does not mean easy. The ordinary kingdom life represents a complete paradigm shift. We have died to ourselves completely, and we now live in Christ completely. Each part of the transformation is all or nothing. That is, Jesus does not ask us to get rid of our top five sins or only gratify our earthly nature Monday through Saturday; he tells us to kill all of it. Nor does Jesus ask us to put on just our favorite parts of his otherworldly values and character. Christ must be our all, or we will end up with nothing.[97]

The great preacher Charles Spurgeon proposed that three things must happen for this paradigm shift to occur, in which Jesus Christ becomes our all. First, Christ must be our source of truth. Second, he must be our source of joy. Third, he must be our great aim. To this list, I will add only one thing: Christ must be our source of identity. Let us examine each of these briefly before moving on to the practical aspects of putting to death distractions and putting on Christ.

Christ as Our Source of Truth

> *We are to follow no man, except so far as he follows Christ, who alone is our Master. Be not deceived; submit not yourselves to creeds, to books, or to men; give yourselves to the study of God's Word, derive your creed and the doctrines of your faith from it alone.*[98]

Christianity is built upon the teachings of the apostles and prophets, with Jesus's teachings serving as the chief cornerstone.[99] Obviously, we will have an extremely difficult, if not impossible, time trying

---

[97] As discussed in the introduction, the kingdom-first pursuit is a pursuit of perfection, not a perfect pursuit. Believers and unbelievers alike continue to sin. The difference between the two is that the former have made God's kingdom rule their preeminent goal and continue to struggle toward that goal, through the power of the Holy Spirit, despite all manner of obstacles and backsliding. The latter, unbelievers, do not struggle. They accept the world's values and reference points as unchangeable "givens" and set about building for themselves earthly kingdoms.

[98] C. H. Spurgeon, "Christ Is All," 1915, access date October 16, 2011, http://www.iclnet.org/pub/resources/text/history/spurgeon/web/ss-0016.html.

[99] Ephesians 2:19–22.

to build God's kingdom if we have never gotten to know our foundation by reading Scripture. Yet many professing Christians make this mistake every day. It seems we would rather piece together our own Jesus from the notions of those around us, regardless of their knowledge base, than to open a Bible and read it for ourselves. Data collected by the Barna Research Group demonstrates this:

> *By a three to one margin (71 percent to 26 percent) adults noted that they are personally more likely to develop their own set of religious beliefs than to accept a comprehensive set of beliefs taught by a particular church. Although born again Christians were among the segments least likely to adopt the a la carte approach to beliefs, a considerable majority even of born again adults (61 percent) has taken that route. Leading the charge in the move to customize one's package of beliefs are people under the age of twenty-five, among whom more than four out of five (82 percent) said they develop their own combination of beliefs rather than adopt a set proposed by a church.[100]*

I am not suggesting that nonconformance to the comprehensive doctrinal standard of a particular local church, by itself, makes one out to be a heretic. However, the result of the "a la carte" approach is often heresy, with us piecing together for ourselves a different god than the God of the Bible. As Barna's Web site points out:

> *Millions of people who consider themselves to be Christian now believe that the Bible is totally accurate in all of the lessons it teaches at the same time that they believe Jesus Christ sinned. Millions also contend that they will experience eternal salvation because they confessed their sins and accepted Christ as their savior, but also believe that a person can do enough good works to earn eternal salvation.[101]*

---

[100] Christianity Is No Longer Americans' Default Faith, Barna Group, Ltd., January 12, 2009, access date January 12, 2009, http://www.barna.org/faith-spirituality/ 15-christianity-is-no-longer-americans-default-faith.

[101] Ibid.

Picking and choosing our way through Scripture according to the whims of our broken hearts is a certain road to hell. There is no way around that. God refuses to let us add or detract from the Bible.[102] We either take Jesus as he is—loving Creator, Redeemer, and King, who rightfully demands preeminence in our lives—or call our new god by a new name. As Scripture warns:

> *Each one should be careful how he builds. For no one can lay any foundation other than the one already laid, which is Jesus Christ.*

> — *1 CORINTHIANS 3:10–11*

It may be helpful to take a moment and test your foundation. Consider reading through the Apostle's Creed or another early Christian confession of faith.[103] Does it describe your beliefs? You can also test yourself by imagining that you are explaining the good news about Jesus to a friend. What would you say? What verses would you use to support what you are saying? What if they asked you hard questions, like why do bad things happen to good people or why do we not follow all the dietary laws in the Old Testament? Where would you go in Scripture?[104]

Christ as Our Source of Identity

> *Here there is no Greek or Jew, circumcised or uncircumcised, barbarian, Scythian, slave or free, but Christ is all, and is in all.*

> —*COLOSSIANS 3:11*

By the very nature of coming to Christ, we will encounter an identity crisis. Apart from Christ we are defined by worldly reference points—black or white, rich or poor, educated or ignorant, beautiful or ugly, talented or otherwise—but in Christ, he alone

---

[102] Deuteronomy 12:32; Revelation 22:18–19.

[103] See Appendix 1 for Apostle's Creed.

[104] See Appendix 2 for practical steps toward knowing Christ through Scripture.

defines us. He alone guides us, and he alone validates our worth. The old labels have no place in the kingdom.

Getting rid of these false identities will not be easy, as the life of a woman I once met illustrates. This woman had a disease called vitiligo, which caused her naturally dark skin to develop patches of light skin. When the patches covered enough of her skin that she could not go anywhere without people staring awkwardly, she elected to undergo a treatment that took the pigment out of the remaining parts of her skin.

This woman talked extensively about the emotional struggle that she and her family went through as her skin color changed from black to white. She told us that her husband had had a hard time being intimate with her anymore because, as he put it, "I married a black woman, not a white woman." It was as if a change of skin color could change who she was as a person.

She went through a similar battle internally. Though you could no longer tell by looking at her, she repeatedly and emphatically referred to herself as a "black woman." She showed myself and others picture after picture of what she used to look like: young, beautiful, and dark-skinned. She could not let go of that image of herself.

When pressed to explain what being black meant beyond a skin color, she struggled to come up with a definition despite its obvious importance to her. In the end she could only say, "I guess I just don't want to be white." Before the vitiligo came, I doubt this woman had any sense of just how much her identity was tied to her skin color. Now she cannot ignore it.

So it is when we come face-to-face with Christ. He will not allow us to cling to our hidden earthly identity but exposes it over and over again, forcing us to choose between it and his otherworldly character.[105] Will we still answer to our self-centered earthly identity, or will we choose instead to live where we live, dress how we dress, work where we work, play what we play, and say what we say all because it is how Christ would live through us for his glory?

---

[105] Matthew 22:2-14.

If we have come through our soul's identity crisis with the firm conviction that Christ is truly all, then it should be a small thing for us to give up the old wardrobe for the new one. This brings to mind a friend who enjoys collecting sports jerseys. His favorite sport is to follow (and play) is soccer, and his favorite team is a Premier League team called Chelsea. I imagine that if my friend was invited to play for Chelsea, he would quickly forget about the dozens of other jerseys he owns.

It would be unthinkable for him to show up to practices or games wearing another team's colors, not merely because of rules, but because his dream of belonging to Chelsea would now be reality, and he would eagerly desire to show the world that reality. All the other jerseys that he owns would become meaningless. As God's dearly loved children, we ought likewise to delight to wear his colors, to be renewed in his image.

Christ as Our Source of Joy

We have already seen how creation was designed to enjoy God as its true King. But this idea can be hard to transfer from intellectual reality to emotive one. Some of that difficulty comes from the fact that we were born into the de-created value system of our broken world, which portrays sin as fun and exciting and holiness as gloomy and somber.

Combine the world's negative marketing of holiness with the language of self-denial and death that comes up repeatedly in Scripture, and it becomes even harder for us to believe that Christians could (or even ought to) be truly happy. So we cling instead to a somber notion of Christian joy, which we convince ourselves is something deeper and more satisfying than happiness and thus has nothing to do with laughter or smiles.

What is missing from this understanding of the Christian life is a proper sense of what we are getting in comparison to what we are giving up. The language in Scripture of death and sacrifice is virtually always accompanied by a promise of reward "that far outweighs" (and thus motivates) the sacrifice.[106] Author C. S. Lewis phrased it this way:

> *The New Testament has lots to say about self-denial, but not about self-denial as an end in itself. We are told to deny ourselves and to take up our crosses in order that we may follow Christ; and nearly every description of what we shall ultimately find if we do so contains an appeal to desire. If there lurks in most modern minds the notion that to desire our own good and earnestly hope for the enjoyment of it is a bad thing, I submit that this notion has crept in from Kant and the Stoics and is no part of the Christian faith. Indeed, if we consider the unblushing promises of reward and the staggering nature of the rewards promised in the Gospels, it would seem that Our Lord finds our desires not too strong, but too weak. We are half-hearted creatures fooling about with drink and sex and ambition when infinite joy is offered to us, like an ignorant child who wants to go on making mud pies in a slum because he cannot imagine what is meant by the offer of a holiday at the sea. We are far too easily pleased.*[107]

As Lewis pointed out, Scripture encourages us to delight in God by reminding us of his loving provision in the future. It also reminds us of those loving provisions made in the past, during creation and on the cross, and of those being provided today through the indwelling of his Spirit.

There is the potential, with all this emphasis on God's provision, that we begin to lose sight of him and focus instead on what he can give us. Many have fallen into this error.[108] Yet the potential for such an error must not be allowed to keep us from seeking happiness in

---

[106] 2 Corinthians 4:17; see also Matthew 13:44–46.

[107] C. S. Lewis, *The Weight of Glory* (New York, NY: HarperCollins, 2001), 25–26.

[108] One example of this is the crowd in John 6:25–70. This crowd had started following Jesus after seeing him heal the sick then followed him across the lake where they were fed miraculously. Now they have followed him in boats across the lake again, revering him as "the prophet" (see Deuteronomy 18:14–19) and desiring to make him king by force. There is no doubt that these are people who have passionately sought after Jesus, yet at the end of the passage only the twelve disciples are left because the crowd was looking for something more than just Jesus. Another example is the "health and wealth" or "prosperity" gospel peddled by many modern-day preachers.

Christ, for delight in him is essential to reflecting his worthiness. As John Piper explains, using the analogy of his wedding anniversary:

> *Suppose on this day I bring home a dozen long-stemmed roses for Noël. When she meets me at the door, I hold out the roses, and she says, "O Johnny, they're beautiful; thank you" and gives me a big hug. Then suppose I hold up my hand and say matter-of-factly, "Don't mention it; it's my duty."*
>
> *What happens? Is not the exercise of duty a noble thing? Do not we honor those we dutifully serve? Not much. Not if there's no heart in it. Dutiful roses are a contradiction in terms. If I am not moved by a spontaneous affection for her as a person, the roses do not honor her. In fact, they belittle her. They are a very thin covering for the fact that she does not have the worth or beauty in my eyes to kindle affection. All I can muster is a calculated expression of marital duty.*[109]

When God is our delight, everything changes. The veil is pulled back on our broken world, and the cracks in our images of success begin to appear. Money and sex and power and talents finally appear as the mud pies that they always were, and rather than envying those around us who have made an end of such things, and bashfully turning down invitations to join in their revelry, we can happily offer them that which is life indeed.

How do we get to that point, though, where intellect and emotions are joined in their delight of God?[110] We must start by realizing that we cannot conjure up joy or happiness in Christ; it is the otherworldly fruit of his Holy Spirit within us.[111] So if we find ourselves lacking delight, we ought to pray with the psalmist,

---

[109] John Piper, *Desiring God* (Sisters, OR: Multnomah Publishers, 2003), 93.

[110] Much of these next two paragraphs is drawn from Appendix 4 of John Piper's *Desiring God*, 351–367.

[111] Galatians 5:22.

"Restore to me the joy of your salvation, and grant me a willing spirit, to sustain me."[112]

Meanwhile we are to strive for joy through the Spirit's power. We do so by regularly reminding ourselves, through reading and reflecting on God's Word, of his abundant provisions as Creator and Redeemer. We also take advantage of the other God-ordained means for encouraging our delight, such as regular rest,[113] fellowship with other believers,[114] and sacrificial service on behalf of others.[115] And when joy still seems far away, we patiently and prayerfully wait,[116] trusting that God is good enough and powerful enough to work through our troubles to provide for us an eternal glory that far outweighs them all.[117]

Christ as Our Great Aim

Here is the practical end of having Jesus Christ as our source of truth, identity, and joy. When he is those things to us, we cannot help but throw ourselves after him with reckless abandonment. In this sense our singular and preeminent pursuit of God's kingdom is much like that of an addict who loses all regard for worldly standards and obligations as his addiction grows, eventually stopping at nothing—potentially losing job, family, and social standing—to satiate his cravings.

This is where many of us get stuck. We cannot make the transition from theoretical to practical, kingdom-first Christianity because we have accepted the lie that our lives naturally compartmentalize into secular and sacred components. This lie, in turn,

---

[112] Psalm 51:12.
[113] Isaiah 58:13–14; John 15:9–13.
[114] Hebrews 3:12–13.
[115] Isaiah 58:10–11.
[116] Psalm 40:1–3.
[117] Romans 8:28; 2 Corinthians 4:17.

leaves us in a hopeless juggling act as we pursue each compartment of our lives as independent and thus competing priorities.[118]

As we saw in chapter one, however, this kind of faith is not biblical. All of life is to be lived for God alone, making use of every part of who we are—living, breathing, thinking, feeling, moving, and doing—to better bear God's image. Until we accept the totality of our call, Christ can never be *the* great aim of our lives. He may become the great aim of our Sunday mornings, our prayers, and our daily Scripture readings, but by themselves those are hardly a worthy throne for the King.

I would guess that few of us, beyond those being paid or otherwise supported to do ministry, have ever thought about how we would build our lives around Christ. So to bring this idea down to earth, imagine the following scenario in which you have just been offered a job in another city. It has everything you ever wanted in terms of scope of practice, pay, benefits, and vacation time. Furthermore, it is exactly what your education and prior work experience have been building towards. In short, it is your dream job.

You quickly accept the offer, as most folks would, and almost simultaneously begin looking for a place to live near that job. Soon enough you have found the ideal location (think of the one you dreamed up in the introduction that is close to work, in a beautiful and safe neighborhood with easy access to high-performing schools and fun recreation opportunities). You put in your offer, it is accepted, and shortly after you (and your family, if you have one) move in.

Before you know it, you have started working. You are eager to make a good impression and thus to secure this dream position, so you do your best to find out what your boss expects, and then do your best to meet or exceed those expectations. This may mean joining committees, taking on extra hours or tasks, and traveling

---

[118] This is the pursuit of *God-and* that I wrote of in the introduction, in which we seek him *and* everything we wanted long before we met him, whether that is health, purpose, morals, family, wealth, community, social network, safety, or any number of other things that we hold as idols in our lives.

to other states or countries, but whatever it is, you enjoy the work so you are happy to comply.

At work you also end up making a handful of good friends. There is nothing too exceptional about these friends, but you are glad to have them considering you left most of your family and friends back home when you moved to start work. Once or twice during the week, you will join them for dinner or to watch television. Almost every weekend you see them again, to enjoy your favorite recreational activity.

After a couple of months of trying out the various local churches, you settle on one to go to. One of your friends from work let you know about it, and after attending a few times you find that it has a similar feel in terms of worship music style and teaching as the one you went to back home, but the coffee is a little better here, which you can appreciate. You also like that it is close to where you live.

In my experience, there is nothing too strange about this scenario. I have seen family and friends go through this basic sequence of events several times. What is interesting is how, without much effort or passage of time, our whole lives—where we live and play and worship and even whom we spend our time with—can become built around our job.

The same centering of details occurs around Christ when he is our great aim. We start with him and build our lives in such a way as to best encourage us to experience and pass on his loving rule. The fact that some places and people must be left behind is no cause for regret, because we are getting the prize we were created to enjoy forever. Indeed, the only reason we spend time thinking about details like where we live, work, play, and worship and whom we spend our time with is because we recognize each as an opportunity to immerse ourselves more fully in the glorious life of the kingdom of heaven.

I am tempted here to offer you a real-life example of what the preeminent pursuit of Christ looks like, something that will make the transition from God-first thinking to God-first living plain to all. Such examples will certainly come, but I hesitate for now because my purpose is not to reproduce in you any particular set of details. Rather, I want each of us to begin the journey of putting off the old self and putting on Christ by looking at our lives just the way they are, full of our ordinary details and our ordinary decisions. This will allow us as individuals to hold ourselves up against the kingdom-first standard and ask, "Is Christ my great aim, or is my life built around other priorities and other gods?"

An Imperfect Pursuit of Perfection

Complete transformation is the spiritual reality of true believers, and in one sense, it is instantaneous. God calls us to himself and declares us righteous and holy in Christ. However, believers still sin. Our goal is perfect godliness, yet our pursuit is decidedly imperfect. We must continually struggle, through the power of the Holy Spirit, to bring our earthly reality in line with our spiritual reality.

In the next part of the book, we will look at the things that belong to our old self, which is our earthly nature. These are the things that distract us from maintaining a single eye on the King; they must be intentionally sought out and methodically "put to death."[119] We should not miss the severity of that command. Sin is at war with us. It desires to master us, and we must respond decisively and aggressively, or be destroyed.[120]

Stripping ourselves of distractions is good, but abstinence from sin, in itself, is hardly a goal. We must go further.[121] We need something to live for, which is what we will find in part three of this book, as we move on to Christ and bearing his image. These attributes are not particular gifts of the Holy Spirit that we can excuse ourselves from; rather, they are the character of the God whose image we bear. To the best of our ability, we put on all of godliness, that we might avoid making an idol of any particular attribute.

---

[119] Colossians 3:5.

[120] Genesis 4:7; 1 Peter 2:11.

[121] Matthew 12:45; Luke 11:26.

As you read along, I encourage you to take an inventory of your life. With each new idea, ask yourself again, "What does it look like for me to seek *first* the kingdom here?" It may be helpful to break that question down a little further into other questions: What in my life adds to my ability (by God's grace) to bear God's image in word and deed? What spurs me on to multiply my faith? What discourages or distracts me from those pursuits?

If, as you are reading along, you find yourself thinking, "I could never do that for God," then please stop and explore the assumption underlying that thought. What would make it impossible? What stands between you and even entertaining the idea of serving God in certain places, in certain ways, under certain circumstances? More than likely, you will find an idol hiding in the shadows of your hesitation, subconsciously limiting your options and directing your steps according to the fallen patterns of this world.

The contents of this book do not represent a new way of doing ministry or life or Christianity. It is the same ordinary kingdom life that God's people have always been called to observe and pass on. However, what is meant to be ordinary Christian living has become foreign to many if not most of us who profess Jesus Christ as our Lord and Savior. Thus, I warn you now, putting off distractions and putting on Christ will require great intentionality and focus expended over years before our thinking and living is renewed such that seeking first his kingdom becomes our default mode of operation as it was meant to be.

II
Putting to Death Distractions

Put to death, therefore, whatever belongs to your earthly nature: sexual immorality, impurity, lust, evil desires and greed, which is idolatry. Because of these, the wrath of God is coming. You used to walk in these ways, in the life you once lived. But now you must rid yourselves of all such things as these: anger, rage, malice, slander, and filthy language from your lips. Do not lie to each other, since you have taken off your old self with its practices and have put on the new self, which is being renewed in knowledge in the image of its Creator. Here there is no Greek or Jew, circumcised or uncircumcised, barbarian, Scythian, slave or free, but Christ is all, and is in all.

—COLOSSIANS 3:5–11

5

Distracted by Sex

Put to death, therefore, whatever belongs to your earthly nature: sexual immorality, impurity, lust...

—*COLOSSIANS 3:5*

In Colossians 3:5 we get our first glimpse of the old self that must be put to death repeatedly this side of eternity. When it comes to potential distractions from kingdom living, I would guess that few have received more negative attention from the church throughout history than sex. Much of this attention is well deserved, given that our ability to pervert God's created order in this area knows no bounds. However, it is worth noting that the negativity has, at times, been so overwhelming that sex itself has been made to seem inherently evil and any desire for it, a regrettable remnant of our earthly nature.

Just to be clear, sex is *not* evil. Rather, it is a gift that was given before sin ever entered into perfect creation, and thus it is to be enjoyed to its fullest extent. As with every gift, though, proper enjoyment requires proper context. In the case of sex, this means one man and one woman becoming "one flesh" in the covenantal relationship of marriage.[122] The intimate and delightful connection between two separate persons, which culminates in the act of sex, serves as a tangible demonstration of divine realities, such as the relationship between Christ and his bride, the church, and the oneness that exists between the three persons of God, as well.[123]

When our marriages lack passion and happiness, we fail to tell God's story properly. As you will recall, creation came about because each person of the Godhead was so overjoyed in one another that they wanted others to experience it, as well. Husbands and wives have the privilege of retelling that story when, out of their mutual delight, they conceive and bear children. These children, in turn, join a family that takes great joy in its members and teaches them to take even greater joy in God.

Because sex is such a wonderful gift, we can be easily distracted by it; and the world, which has plenty to say about sex and its role in our life, is only too happy to help lead us astray. In very general terms, sex becomes a distraction, or false reference point, when we pursue it primarily for any one of the following: pleasure, identity, relationship, or procreation. We will examine these one by one and then move on to consider what it might look like to use the kingdom of heaven as the lone reference point for our sexuality.

Sex for Pleasure's Sake

We do not have to look far to find this false reference point. Popular magazines, available in any grocery store checkout line, promise us dozens of "new" and "naughty" sex positions. Ads for sexual enhancements—herbal supplements, prescriptions drugs, more sensitive condoms, and stimulating lubricants—bombard us from every form media. Whole stores are devoted to lingerie. Parties are thrown to demonstrate and sell sex toys. These are the patterns of our world, tempting us to make sexual pleasure an end in itself.

---

[122] Genesis 2:18–25; 1 Corinthians 7:2.
[123] Ephesians 5:22–32.

When we accept sexual pleasure as our primary reference point, God is placed in conflict with his gift. Like our first parents, we are tricked into thinking that God is holding us back from the one thing that will make us truly happy. If we cling to our doubt of God's goodness, despite the promises of Scripture, we have two options: we can obey the outward letter of the law, while rotting away inside, or we can choose outright disobedience.[124]

If we choose to hide our doubt, it may go unnoticed for a time, but at the same time, it will grow unchecked. That man from the gym may never know that his body occupies our daydreams, nor will the woman from the movie who made love the way we wish our wife did. Our friend may not catch our eyes lingering over her low-cut shirt or her spring break photos online, and our coworker who makes us laugh and feel beautiful, the way our husband once did, might not realize how we ache for his companionship. But hidden sin is still sin, and more than likely, it will eventually work itself out in very visible ways.

Open disregard for God's plan leads to self-directed experimentation and sexual immorality in all its various forms—fornication, adultery, homosexuality, prostitution, rape, abuse, or bestiality.[125] This is where, historically, the church's focus has been in eliminating sexual sin. In the name of tolerance, however, many churches in our day have swung to the opposite pole and stopped calling out sin and demanding repentance altogether, choosing instead to affirm sinners in whatever they do. Thus, many faithful churchgoers are left thinking that the sexual pleasure they find in extramarital affairs, same gender relationships, live-in boyfriends, and permanent fiancées supersedes any antiquated command from Scripture.

---

[124] In choosing outright disobedience, you would think our rebellion would be obvious even to ourselves. However, we often blind ourselves that reality by changing our beliefs about God to better fit our desires.

[125] Incest (Leviticus 18:6; Deuteronomy 27:20, 22), fornication (Numbers 25:1, 6; 1 Samuel 2:22), adultery (2 Samuel 11:4; John 4:17–18), rape (Genesis 34:1–2; 2 Samuel 13:10–14), homosexuality (Leviticus 18:22; 20:13; Romans 1:26–27), prostitution (Deuteronomy 23:18), and bestiality (Deuteronomy 27:21). Adapted, with references, from D. R. W. Wood and I. H. Marshall, *New Bible Dictionary*, 3rd ed. (Leicester, England; Downers Grove, IL: InterVarsity Press, 1996), 211–212.

What about you and me? Are we content in God's design for, and limitations on, our sexuality, or do we entertain doubts about him? Do we believe that God truly wants us to be happy and is capable of making us so? Do we trust him to provide everything (including that wonderful spouse for whom we physically and emotionally ache) to us in its most delightful form and time? If doubts arise, what do we do with them?

Sex for Identity's Sake

For the Christian there is no identity apart from Christ. As we have seen before:

> *Here there is no Greek or Jew, circumcised or uncircumcised, barbarian, Scythian, slave or free, but Christ is all, and is in all.*

> —*COLOSSIANS 3:11*

That is, of course, not what sinners want to hear or tell each other. Whether it is through our sexuality, intellect, or talents, we long for an identity that is our own. For many, this issue of identity revolves around labels such as heterosexual, homosexual, bisexual, asexual, or transgender.

The problem is not so much that we have desires for men or women or both, but that we take our cues from our self-constructed sexual identities. For example, if we are attracted to members of the opposite sex, then we do things that we think heterosexual folks do. On the other hand, if we are attracted to members of the same sex, then we do things that we think homosexual folks do.

By identifying ourselves according to sexual orientation, we have set our sexual preferences above the encouragement and rebuke of others. "It is how God made me," our logic flows. "Therefore, how could it be wrong?" This misses the reality that, in our fallen state, sin is what seems most natural to us. De-creation is the air we breathe and the water we swim in, so to speak, and thus our consciences prove unreliable apart from an objective standard of holiness.

As Creator, God has the authority to tell us, his creation, what we were and were not made to do and think. If we are willing to follow his commands to put to death our desires to steal, kill, rape, and destroy, which also spring from our earthly nature, should we not also be willing to put to death our misplaced sexual desires?

Sex for Relationship's Sake

In the proper context, sex is an exquisite expression *of* intimate and abiding love. One of the more subtle falsities of our world is to turn that reality on its head and portray sex as the means *to* intimate and abiding love. Perhaps we have heard someone ask, for example, "How can you really know if you are compatible with someone unless you have lived with him or her and shared a bed first?" Maybe we have even had a friend sleep with her boyfriend just to keep him around and interested.

The desires to feel loved and express devotion are not wrong. They are beautiful remnants of our perfect created state, and there are many ways, short of sex, to express them as one single person to another. The question is this: Are our eyes fixed on a God who both desires and is able to provide for us, or is our god spiteful and weak? If we choose to use sex out of turn, as a means of securing a relationship, then be assured that we have chosen the latter and lesser god.

Sex for Procreation's Sake

This last false reference point is, at times, obviously wrong and, at others, much more subtle in its error. For example, imagine the single mother on government assistance for whom an additional child brings with it the promise of additional income. What disciple of Christ would encourage her to find a boyfriend simply to get pregnant? Now, imagine the young married couple who sees having children as *the* means of filling and subduing the earth on God's behalf. In contrast to the situation of the single mother, few Christians would likely object to the holy-appearing intentions of this pair.

We should object, though, for there are at least two problems with the young couple's view of procreation. First, it misconstrues the means by which we are commanded to build God's kingdom. Remember, in a fallen world, multiplication of God's rule means passing along our singular love for God through intentional discipleship. This may include having kids, biologically or otherwise, and it may not. Second, it places such a premium on having kids that sex inevitably becomes a passionless duty and loses its ability to bear witness to the glorious and intimate relationship of Christ and the church

Sex for the Kingdom's Sake

Now that we have examined a handful of the false reference points the world offers, let us consider what it might look like to use the kingdom of heaven as the reference point for our sexuality. While some of the specific applications will vary quite a bit from person to person, one thing is not negotiable in God's kingdom: a singular love for God that obeys and multiplies. Thus, when God says sex is a gift to be enjoyed only inside of a marriage between one man and one woman, his would-be disciples have to ask a few questions of themselves:

- Do my thoughts, words, and deeds demonstrate delightful submission to God's plan?
- What can I do to better encourage my own joy-filled obedience to God's plan?
- What can I do to encourage the same delight for God's ways in others?

As we think through these questions, we would do well to do two things. First, we need to clean our eyes out by setting aside all our notions of sexuality and purpose in life. Second, we need to fix our eyes on God's reality. Let his nature become our natural—forgoing all other paths to sexual pleasure—that we might enjoy sex as it was meant to be enjoyed, thoroughly and for God's glory.

If we are currently single, good! We can make the most of it by serving in times, ways, and places that are harder for married folks. We ought not waste ourselves thinking or complaining about what we do not have or escape into romance novels or movies or pornography. Instead, we ought to develop our relationship with our loving Creator by reading his Word and praying to him. And we should do so with joy, setting ourselves apart from those who would make an idol of relationships.

If we desire marriage, good! This, too, is a gift and one we should prepare for by rooting ourselves all the more in Christ and maturing in him, lest we be distracted from his kingdom by the one we choose to pursue and love. When it comes to finding a partner, we need to find a man or woman who truly puts God first. Everything else is just frosting. So instead of starting your search with qualifiers such as looks, talents, and shared hobbies, look for a spouse who treasures Christ with his or her life and invests the time, talent, and resources he or she has been given for his kingdom.

If we have found (or been found by) someone of marriageable character but are not yet married to this person, then we need to be patient. The promise of sexual pleasure is wonderful, and it can be easy to want to skip ahead. But sex is not better than Christ, nor is it so great that we cannot wait another minute or day or week or even year without experiencing it. Setting clear boundaries in our relationship and inviting friends to keep us accountable to such boundaries can be helpful. But boundaries do nothing to constrain our hearts. We still have to struggle, in all of God's incomparable power, to keep our eyes on Christ rather than on maintaining an appearance of morality.

If we do move on to marriage, then we need to leave our birth family and cleave to our spouse.[126] We should enjoy our husband or wife—physically, emotionally, and spiritually—to the fullest extent and so bear witness to the loving provision of the Lord. It will help tremendously if we can learn to delight in the things that

---

[126] Genesis 2:24.

bring our spouse delight and develop sincere and passionate devotion to him or her. We can share our joy with the world by learning to genuinely praise our spouse in the presence of others. If there are obstacles to delighting in one another, however harmless or humiliating they seem, we must rid ourselves of them by confessing sin to one another and forgiving each other.

We need also be mindful to encourage joyful submission in the lives and hearts of others with both our words and our deeds. We can take no delight in the world's cheap perversions of God's plan, whether it be by laughing along with the lewd jokes of another, agreeing by virtue of silence, or by chasing after such things ourselves. With non-Christians, we should make it our aim to share the incomparable worth of Christ, reserving any expectations of obedience for the professing Christians around us.

On the other hand, if a brother or sister in Christ is violating God's clear teachings on sex, we are not only to remind them of Christ's worth, but to gently and humbly rebuke them. We must continue to do so as long as that person continues to claim Christ. In gray areas, however, where sin is not clearly defined, we must give others the freedom to have different convictions than us.[127]

In the end, what we do with our bodies is not up to us. As Creator and Redeemer, Jesus owns us twice over.[128] He is our Master, and he gets to call all the shots. We can take great comfort in that reality because we know that he is not out to get us. The abundant provisions of creation assure us of God's love, and all the more his willingness to die for us, while we were still his enemies. Where God places certain limits on us, his desire is always to maximize his glory and, consequently, our joy.[129]

---

[127] This does not mean that we cannot approach them if we are concerned about their direction, but we cannot make our boundaries (no matter how useful they are to us) into laws for others to follow.

[128] 1 Corinthians 6:19–20.

[129] It seems the least helpful thing God can do for us is to allow us to chase, uninhibited, after our fallen desires (Romans 1:18–32).

6

Distracted by Money

Put to death...greed, which is idolatry.

—Colossians 3:5

Greed is the selfish desire for more wealth and possessions than is needed to sustain life and ministry. It is the second false reference point that we will examine from Paul's list. What is interesting about wealth, or money, is that it can be a distraction by itself or the means by which we pursue any number of other distractions. Thus, a careful review of our spending is often the quickest and surest way to track down our idols. For, as Jesus said, "Where our treasure is, there our heart will be also."[130]

Still, it is important to remember that money itself is not evil. It is a neutral object that can, like every detail in life, be used in ways that further God's rule (i.e., Christian stewardship), or detract from it (i.e., greed). See how Paul contrasts these two approaches:

---

[130] Luke 12:34.

Godliness with contentment is great gain. For we brought nothing into the world, and we can take nothing out of it. But if we have food and clothing, we will be content with that. People who want to get rich fall into temptation and a trap and into many foolish and harmful desires that plunge men into ruin and destruction. For the love of money is a root of all kinds of evil. Some people, eager for money, have wandered from the faith and pierced themselves with many griefs.

—*1 Timothy 6:6–10*

Godliness with contentment is what Jesus expects of his followers and disciples, and we will explore what that looks like at the end of the chapter. However, let us first consider the love of money and how it works itself out in a handful of the more prevalent and celebrated money-related distractions among professing Christians of our day.

Money for Pleasure's Sake

At the root of all sin is a misconception of ownership. You see, if we are our own, then we have the right to do whatever we want with ourselves and with whatever resources we possess: our car, our house, our clothes, our food, and our money that paid for them all. On the other hand, if we are God's creation, then we have no rights at all and no possessions to speak of, either.

If pressed, most professing Christians would probably agree with the idea that everything we commonly refer to as *ours* is truly *God's*. However, it seems that few folks approach life according to this reality. At best, we will give God a certain percentage of our income, and at worst (and quite commonly), we give him nothing. The part we keep, whether it be ninety percent or one hundred percent, we consider our own, to be used by us according to our good pleasure.

The problem is not that we enjoy life, but that we see money as the primary means of obtaining joy for ourselves. With a little bit more, we could play more golf, take more vacations, buy a fancier car, or move into a bigger house in a safer neighborhood. Maybe we could also afford the cottage and boat we always wanted or, better yet, retire early. If we only had a little more, the lie goes, then we might finally be happy.

If we have compartmentalized our lives into secular and spiritual pursuits, it may be easy to convince ourselves that God is indifferent to our secular expenditures so long as we give him a little from time to time. However, we will still run into the problem of having set our pleasure in competition with God's kingdom. Cheerful and sacrificial giving, as commended in Scripture,[131] is no longer possible, for we cannot ever bring ourselves to give so much that it would cost us the next thing on our wish list.[132]

Money for Identity's Sake

Whether we like it or not, what we eat, drink, and wear sends messages to others about who we are. Most of us instinctively understand this and have been manipulating those details subconsciously for years to project a certain image of ourselves to others. That is, for example, why when we show up to a job interview, we tend to clean up a little and wear our best suit, shirt, tie, and shoes.

Of course, potential bosses are the least of our worries. There are dozens of other people, if not hundreds, we come across on a daily basis. How do we identify ourselves to them? Do we present ourselves as those who are wealthy, intellectual, cool, athletic, artistic, married, attractive, cultured, or easygoing? How much money do we spend on our clothes, jewelry, hairstyle, car, recreational activities, and gadgets to achieve the desired effect?

---

[131] Exodus 25:2; 1 Chronicles 29:9, 17; 2 Corinthians 8:12; 9:7.

[132] This kind of idolatry is easier to hide when one has plenty of money because the wealthier we become, the more we can give without truly giving anything up.

Maintaining an identity through money does not have to be a conscious process, nor is it always wrapped up in having money. Whether we are part of the upper, middle, or lower class, most of us spend our lives within a socioeconomic group with well-established norms regarding resources. Though we could not say exactly why, we demand a certain type of job or car or house or clothes or entertainment. If a product does not meet those standards, we either refuse to buy it or find ways, like with a house, of updating it to meet our perceived needs.

The problem is not that we end up accepting a high-paying job or that we buy name-brand jeans. Rather, our problem is that, despite the warning of Jesus that "a man's life does not consist in the abundance of his possessions,"[133] we define ourselves in socioeconomic terms and make these decisions (about jobs and jeans) based on an earthly reference point of who we want to be. We place at least part of our identity in possessions, and thus Christ cannot be our all.

Starting with any reference point but Christ's kingdom effectively precludes us from doing whatever we do for his glory. We are approaching the Christian life with half a menu, so to speak, because by using our socioeconomic references points first, we have already cut the options in two. One list is made up of things we will not do or wear or places we will not live, and the other list, which we are willing to choose from, is made up of those things we are still happy to do and wear and places we could still imagine ourselves living. In the end, Christ is left with the scraps of our time, talent, and treasure being put to work in his service.

Money for Security's Sake

> *Earthly goods are given to be used, not to be collected...If {the disciple} stores {his portion} up as a permanent possession, he spoils not only the gift, but himself as well, for he sets his heart on his accumulated wealth, and makes it a barrier between himself and*

---

[133] Luke 12:15.

God. Where our treasure is, there is our trust, our security, our consolation and our God.[134]

Despite strong warnings from Christians down through the ages, few idols have met with such widespread acceptance and praise, among professing Christians, as the security of self-sufficiency. This often begins under the guise of stewardship, with sound financial wisdom leading to freedom from debt and the ability to provide for the needs of oneself and one's family. However, the principle of stewardship can easily be twisted into the gospel of preservation and accumulation, which promises peace of mind to its disciples independent of God.

Worrying about what we eat, drink, and wear not only today or tomorrow, but next month or next year, is all very practical. It makes good earthly sense that we should buy insurance policies and put aside money into emergency funds and rainy-day accounts. It also makes good earthly sense that if we think we might not be able to (or want to) work in ten to fifteen years, then we should start saving up now to provide for ourselves in the future.

It is worth at least considering, however, if all of our risk-averse pragmatism is indeed godly. That is, does it lead us to put our faith in God or ourselves? I cannot help but imagine that Jesus was challenging us to something greater than earthly common sense when he spoke the words:

> *Therefore I tell you, do not worry about your life, what you will eat; or about your body, what you will wear. Life is more than food, and the body more than clothes. Consider the ravens: They do not sow or reap, they have no storeroom or barn; yet God feeds them. And how much more valuable you are than birds! Who of you by worrying can add a single hour to his life? Since you cannot do this very little thing, why do you worry about the rest?*

---

[134] Dietrich Bonhoeffer, *The Cost of Discipleship* (New York, NY: Touchstone, 1995), 175.

Consider how the lilies grow. They do not labor or spin. Yet I tell you, not even Solomon in all his splendor was dressed like one of these. If that is how God clothes the grass of the field, which is here today, and tomorrow is thrown into the fire, how much more will he clothe you, O you of little faith! And do not set your heart on what you will eat or drink; do not worry about it. For the pagan world runs after all such things, and your Father knows that you need them. But seek his kingdom, and these things will be given to you as well.

Do not be afraid, little flock, for your Father has been pleased to give you the kingdom. Sell your possessions and give to the poor. Provide purses for yourselves that will not wear out, a treasure in heaven that will not be exhausted, where no thief comes near and no moth destroys. For where your treasure is, there your heart will be also.

—LUKE 12:22–34

Jesus's answer to our worries is to seek first God's kingdom and trust him, our loving Heavenly Father, to take care of the details for us. What a wonderful promise! Yet how often we misunderstand it and so quickly dismiss it on pragmatic grounds: "That is all well and good," we say, "but if I do not get a job and pay my bills, then who will take care of me?" or, even more poignantly, "Who will take care of my kids?" Such questions are not bad, but they do miss the point of the passage.

Jesus's point is not that we give up our job or stop providing for our family. Neither does he address how God will take care of us, though it can be argued, from other passages, that it is primarily through his people.[135] Rather, Jesus is demanding of us a worry-free existence, focused on God's kingdom rather than our circumstances.

---

[135] Matthew 19:29; Mark 10:29; Luke 18:29; 2 Corinthians 8:1–15.

When we focus on our circumstances first, we panic and lose sight of God's plan altogether. Satan takes advantage of our panic and presents us with options that seem very practical and promise us peace. Yet in reality, these options lead us down paths that open us up to ungodly influences and detract from our ability to expand God's rule.

Take Abraham, for example. God called him to move to the land of Canaan to start a new nation. When he arrived in Canaan, Abraham discovered that the land was in the middle of a famine. So, rather than stay in the place to which he was called, he made a very practical decision to head to Egypt where he knew there would be enough food for him and his family to survive. In Egypt, Abraham made some more very practical, yet ungodly, decisions to lie and prostitute out his wife for fear that the Egyptians would harm him if they knew the truth.

Imagine yourself in a similar position where you had to move with your company to another part of the country, just to keep your job in a time of recession. Would you go? If you did, would you do the legwork necessary to decide beforehand whether such a move would challenge you to grow in godliness and to make disciples? Even after such an analysis, would you or I turn down the job simply because it is does not add to our pursuit of the kingdom of God?

I wonder how many of us have ended up like Abraham (or his nephew Lot, or Ruth's father-in-law, Elimelech, for that matter[136]) discovering days, months, or even years later the devastating spiritual results of our earthly pragmatism? Do we even make the connection between the decision and the results, or are we so naïve to the effect of our decisions on our pursuit of God that we are left dumbfounded by their aftermath and chalk up our backsliding to chance?

---

[136] Both Lot and Elimelech (Genesis 19:1–37 and Ruth 1:1–5, respectively) made decisions to move away from God's people to places where they would be without godly influence. They did so without regard for extending God's heavenly rule on earth. Lot moved because he saw that the land was good and Elimelech because there was a famine in his hometown of Bethlehem. While these decisions seem reasonable enough, both men's stories end with their families being overrun by the influences of the world around them and their children marrying or being promised in marriage to pagans.

y for the Kingdom's Sake

Jesus's teaching, in Luke 12:22–34, not only exposes our misplaced sense of security but gives us a great starting point for answering this question: "What does it look like to use God's kingdom as our primary reference point for deciding how we spend or save money?" If we were created to be God's stewards and everything we tend to think of as our own truly belongs to Jesus, how do we make that transition to seeing our car, our house, and our money as, in reality, his house, his car, and his money?

From other teachings of Jesus, like the parable of the talents, we know that we are not to try to preserve what we have been given, but to use it in ways that bear eternal rewards.[137] This parable is only helpful, though, if we understand what constitutes an "eternal reward." Is it a pile of heavenly money, for example, or a heavenly mansion or perhaps a closer spot to the King? While this question may seem trivial at first, knowing the answer is crucial to wisely investing our lives and our resources today.

For insight into the nature of our reward, consider another parable that Jesus told of a servant found to be wasting his master's possessions.[138] Realizing that he will soon be fired, the servant decides to the make the most of his last few hours to provide for his future. So he arranges for all the folks who owe his master money to come, and one by one, he decreases the amount each debtor owes. In doing so, the servant ensures that he will have friends who will look out for him after he loses his job.

Jesus's take-home point at the end of this parable is this: "Use worldly wealth to gain friends for yourselves, so that when it is gone, you will be welcomed into eternal dwellings."[139] Such friends, who can welcome us in eternity, are none other than fellow believers who have likewise set their minds and hearts on the King. Since believers are

---

[137] Matthew 25:14–30.

[138] Luke 16:1–15.

[139] Luke 16:9.

"gained" by "making" disciples, the call to use earthly wealth to store up treasures in heaven is the call to fund the work of discipleship.[140]

At the most basic level, people need food, clothing, and shelter to sustain the life required to share, hear, and respond to the Word of God. Providing for these needs is as important as providing for the costs of organized ministry, whether that be a local body with a pastor and a meeting place, printing Bibles, or sending missionaries to the far corners of the earth.

For most of us, funding discipleship starts by acquiring an honest job that allows us to earn money to pay for our basic needs.[141] Once we have a job and are making money, then we have the privilege of deciding how to invest God's money. Here, kingdom priority implies a distinct chronological order. Before God's people provide for their own needs, they set aside their first and best for God, to be given to him directly. This is what we commonly refer to as tithes.

God's people have always been expected to give him the firstfruits of their labor.[142] This was and is the means by which we support the people whose job it is to carry out the organized worship of God. By giving our first and best fruits, rather than just any old fruits, we not only provide (in our day) for pastors and missionaries and campus ministry staff, but we also demonstrate tangibly our trust in the King to continue to provide for us after the initial harvest.

While most of us have heard of tithing, which literally means giving 10 percent, it may surprise us to know that when we add up all the "tithes" God asked for from his people, it accounts for upwards of 25 percent of their income.[143] That kind of giving is hard to imagine considering how low we set our bar today, if we set one

---

[140] God does not need any money to bring the world under his control. He could easily do it through visions and epiphanies. But according to his good pleasure, he chooses instead to use us to go and make disciples, and he has provided us with more than enough resources to ensure that we can do so.

[141] 1 Thessalonians 4:11; 2 Thessalonians 3:10–12. Anyone who can work to provide for himself and his family but chooses not to do so is worse than an unbeliever and should not be given handouts (1 Timothy 5:8; 2 Thessalonians 3:10).

[142] Exodus 23:19; Leviticus 23:10; Numbers 3:13; Nehemiah 10:35; Romans 8:23; James 1:18; Revelation 14:4.

[143] Driscoll and Breshears, *Doctrine*, 393.

at all. To put things in perspective, consider that only 27 percent of evangelicals clear the traditional 10 percent bar in their tithing. Meanwhile, more than one-quarter of American Protestants give nothing. Overall that amounts to an annual median tithe, for self-identified Christians, of a meager two hundred dollars. That ends up being only 0.5 percent of after tax income, a full fifty times less than God's people before us were expected to give![144]

Let us move on from tithes. What we do with the rest of the money is just as important as what we do with the first part. After we have given our first and best, then we determine our needs. In the kingdom of heaven, need is not measured by mere physical survival nor by what keeps us comfortable and financially secure. Instead, need is determined by whatever options—clothing, housing, food, career, transportation, family size, education, and recreation—best encourage us to share the good news about Jesus, in word and deed, to those around us.

Driven by the desire to see the kingdom of God grow in times and places, godly stewards are always looking for ways to do more with less, that they might spread more of God's wealth out to those around them. Such giving is not done haphazardly,[145] but with the conscious intent of expanding God's rule both through organized discipleship efforts, such as churches or missionaries, and through efforts that reflect God's generous compassion, by providing for the basic needs of those who cannot provide for themselves.[146]

God gives generously so that his disciples can show the world, in word and deed, the love of Christ.[147] Rather than asking self-centered questions such as "How much house, car, television, cell phone, or computer can I afford?" we should be asking kingdom-first questions like, "Where is God moving, and how can I put more of my resources behind those efforts?" This is for God's glory and our good, as John Piper explains:

---

[144] Driscoll and Breshears, *Doctrine*, 396–397.

[145] Deuteronomy 18:4; 1 Corinthians 16:1–2.

[146] Deuteronomy 15:11; Luke 6:35; 2 Corinthians 8:13–15.

[147] 2 Corinthians 9:8–13.

We can be content with the necessities of life because the deepest, most satisfying delights God gives us through creation are free gifts from nature and loving relationships with people. After your basic needs are met, money begins to diminish your capacity for these pleasures rather than increase them. Buying things contributes absolutely nothing to the heart's capacity for joy.[148]

Kingdom-inspired simplicity and generosity are our safeguards against the deceits of wealth, meant to keep us running unhindered along the straight and narrow path of discipleship to Jesus.[149] To make use of such safeguards, however, we must do more than simply give of our excess. As Paul exhorted the believers in Corinth:

And now, brothers, we want you to know about the grace that God has given the Macedonian churches. Out of the most severe trial, their overflowing joy and their extreme poverty welled up in rich generosity. For I testify that they gave as much as they were able, and even beyond their ability. Entirely on their own, they urgently pleaded with us for the privilege of sharing in this service to the saints. And they did not do as we expected, but they gave themselves first to the Lord and then to us in keeping with God's will.

— 2 CORINTHIANS 8:1–5

God's goal in these examples is not to promote poverty but equality among believers. As Paul goes on to say:

At the present time your plenty will supply what they need, so that in turn their plenty will supply what you need. Then there will be

---

[148] John Piper, "Money: Currency for Christian Hedonism," sermon delivered on October 9, 1983, at Bethlehem Baptist Church in Minneapolis, Minnesota, www.desiringgod.org.

[149] 1 Timothy 6:17–19.

equality, as it is written: "He who gathered much did not have too much, and he who gathered little did not have too little."

—2 Corinthians 8:14–15

We do not stumble into the kind of rich generosity that is required to provide for the needs of other believers and members of the body of Christ. It takes great intentionality and frequent spurring on from fellow believers to not only plan for such generosity but to follow through with our plans, because our current default mode of operation is to put our needs ahead of those around us.

Those of us who have more than we need (which is probably almost everyone reading this book) would do well to consider setting a cap on our expenditures at the level required to maintain our own ministry, including the daily needs of food, shelter, and clothing. Everything else would be invested in God's kingdom in some form or another, providing us with the delight of seeing our fellow believers equipped to reach the lost around them. Such a cap could be easily adjusted as our own ministry, and the ministries we give to, change over time.

Let us also consider moving past our bank accounts and taking an inventory of our possessions. What things do we need to minister to our local body and community? How does that compare to what we have? What things do we own that detract from our ability to bear God's image and make disciples who do the same? What can we give away or sell—clothes, tools, cars, computers, houses, books, appliances, furniture, and so forth—to provide for the needs of others?

For most, if not all of us, putting God first in the area of resources will involve giving something up. Our spending will change, and our joy-sapping load of possessions will be lightened. As we develop new convictions and creative, kingdom-building strategies, we would do well to let a trusted Christian friend take a look at our finances and our resources and keep us accountable to implementing our ideas.[150]

Christian stewardship will look strange indeed to the world around us. We will be considered fools for squandering our resources on others, who may or may not be grateful for what we offer them. Even within the professing church, folks will not always understand us. They will call us irresponsible for giving until it hurts, well beyond what the world considers our ability.

Yet, at the same time, the world and the professing church will be getting a glimpse of God's generosity through us. We will become as the Macedonians to the Corinthians, and we will enjoy the reward of the faithful. Never forget the reward.[151] Eternal life with the risen King Jesus belongs to those who die daily to the finite life of comfort and opulence offered us by money. We cannot serve both God and money, so whom will we choose? How will that choice work itself out in our budget today?

---

[150] As we are developing our convictions, we must learn to strike that godly balance between extending our individual applications into a requirement for others and yet still holding other Christians—particularly our leaders (1 Timothy 3:2–3; 8–9)—accountable to be free of the love of money.

[151] Matthew 19:27–30; 2 Corinthians 4:16–17.

7

Distracted by Evil Desires

"Put to death...evil desires."

—*COLOSSIANS 3:5*

"Evil desires" is a somewhat nebulous category. Although this generality initially makes direct application to our lives more difficult, it also reminds us that our goal in reading Scripture is not to come up with any exhaustive list of clear, or black-and-white, sins to avoid. Rather, we ought to be so comfortable with our kingdom-first reference point that we can use it to guide every decision, even those in life's gray areas, measuring each by how it adds or detracts from our ability to be image bearers who multiply.

Clearly sex and money are not the only things in life that can distract us from seeking first God's kingdom. Given the chance, anything and everything can distract—even those things that seem to be inherently good and have a proper place in kingdom living. Family can distract us, as can work, recreation, service, evangelism, and even writing books about God and how to live for him.

Whatever hinders our allegiance to Jesus must be thrown off so that we may fix our eyes solely on our King.

Even our worldly obligations are not spared from the God-first call. Jesus made sure his first followers understood that reality clearly, so that they might decide for themselves whether God was worth it or not.[152]

As they were walking along the road, a man said to him, "I will follow you wherever you go."

Jesus replied, "Foxes have holes and birds of the air have nests, but the Son of Man has no place to lay his head."

He said to another man, "Follow me."

But the man replied, "Lord, first let me go and bury my father."

Jesus said to him, "Let the dead bury their own dead, but you go and proclaim the kingdom of God."

Still another said, "I will follow you, Lord; but first let me go back and say good-by to my family."

Jesus replied, "No one who puts his hand to the plow and looks back is fit for service in the kingdom of God."

—LUKE 9:57–62

Those kinds of words are devastating to our earthly nature, and rightfully so. Continuing to embrace false reference points when God has called us to a singular and preeminent gaze on his loving rule is not just unproductive; it is evil. If our tendency is to only ever look for really ugly sins to put to death, we will, like the men

---

[152] See also Luke 14:25–35.

above, miss the false reference points right in front of us that keep us from wholehearted pursuit of Christ.

With the idea of bringing some of these hidden distractions out into the open, let us walk together through another list of reference points. These false reference points do not make it into Paul's list in Colossians, but are nevertheless readily evident in our conversations, actions, and justifications. This is not an attempt to extend anyone's checklist of sins, but rather to offer a starting point, full of examples from which we can begin to explore the evil desires of our individual hearts and the misplaced affections that underlie some of our most ingrained assumptions.

As you read along, I encourage you to try on the various false reference points to see if they fit your heart and your experience. Consider asking yourself some of these questions: What have I placed alongside of God? Where have I made good things into god things? Am I trying to balance any of these with "Jesus's part" of my life? How would my thoughts, actions, and words change if I were to put God first in this area?[153]

You may find your idolatrous reference point(s) among those in this list, and you may not. Either way, keep searching, leaving no corner of your heart, mind, or life untouched.

Career

A job can distract us in any number of ways. It can, just as we saw with sex and socioeconomics, come to define us in a way that only King Jesus should. Though it may seem trivial, consider how we introduce ourselves to others. Are we not so often nurses and lawyers and builders and musicians and pastors, long before we are Christians? If it were limited to introductions, that would be one thing, but often it is not.

---

[153] Questions like these challenge the status quo of our lives, threatening to upset the balance that we have struck between our various gods. If we do not ask such questions, however, we (and whomever we try to disciple) are in grave danger of assuming that we have a God-first heart, when we do not. In that case, we will find ourselves walking up to King Jesus one day and hearing the awful words, "I never knew you. Away from me, you evildoers" (Matthew 7:23).

Some of us are guilty of using our profession as the dominant priority in deciding how we should think, act, dress, speak, and otherwise spend God's resources. As we saw in chapter four, we often treat our job as the only given in life, the one thing that all other details are built around. This can be true even before we begin to work full-time.

For example, how many of us would think twice about moving to pursue an education at a higher-ranked school, with the idea of having more job opportunities at the end of the day? How many of us have likewise chosen, or still regularly choose, studying over opportunities for service, evangelism, or fellowship, again with the idea in mind that we must get the highest grade possible to secure that ideal job?

Instead of seeing employment as our top priority, what would it look like to pursue a job in a way that encourages our real priority: godly obedience in ourselves and in those around us? Would we stay in the same place, with the same job, with the same company? Would we put the same emphasis on education, college rankings, or notoriety when it comes to choosing and preparing for a career? How might things go differently?

Humanity

For others of us, there is no higher purpose in life than the betterment of humanity. Focusing on this false reference point leads us to put our time, talents, and treasure to use, improving the world around us. This becomes problematic when our desire to see change leads us to concentrate on the tangible (and more easily manipulated) aspects of folks' lives. In this case, betterment is not so much measured by extending God's rule in people's hearts as it is in bringing an end to the ravages of poverty, war, and disease, and ushering in peace, diversity, tolerance, sustainability, and economic development to the neediest members of our global community.

Such activities are wonderful, but they make horrible goals in and of themselves, because they create an imbalanced approach to kingdom building that emphasizes ministering through deeds over ministering through words. Yes, Jesus expects us to meet the physical needs of those around us. Yet, at the *same* time (without sacrificing any of our concern for physical needs) we are to be speaking gospel truth into our neighbors' lives to meet their spiritual needs as well. For, as Jesus taught, "Man does not live on bread alone but on every word that comes from the mouth of the Lord."[154]

Country

When you love your country as much or more than you love God, the results can be obvious, or they can be quite subtle. If you live in a country where government-sanctioned persecution of Christians occurs, then siding with your country will clearly set you at odds with God's people, as you either openly join in their abuse or passively consent to such treatment by your silence. On the other hand, if you live in a place where Christians go about unopposed, then you may be able to juggle your faith quite nicely with your patriotic loyalties.

Of course, a shift in policy is all it really takes to expose the duplicity of a nominal church clinging to its country a little harder than it is to God. Take, for example, the German church of the 1930s. When Adolf Hitler came to power, he swept the nation (including the bulk of the German church) off its feet with passionate appeals to national pride and sense of civic duty. Their devotion to country was such that, when Hitler openly turned on the Jewish people, the German church, largely, did nothing to stop him. Instead, it continued to openly support his regime.

While Nazi Germany makes a convenient scapegoat, the duplicity of its established church is not unheard of in modern America. In the wake of the terrorist attacks of September 11, 2001, patriotism has enjoyed renewed vigor both inside and outside of our churches. Flags adorn churches and, in some cases, even altars. Rather than consider ourselves as aliens and strangers in this land, we often unite our country with our Lord, imagining that the United States is somehow a Christian nation that enjoys special favor with God.

---

[154] Deuteronomy 8:3; Matthew 4:4.

Sadly, this blurs the line between America's goals and God's, and picking up a flag becomes as good as picking up a cross.

Could it be that our inability to distinguish between the two is why some fight so hard to keep phrases like "In God we trust" or "one nation under God" as part of our national credo? Maybe it is also why others love to sing, with hymn-like reverence, songs like "God Bless America" that tie the two reference points into one and set up America's prosperity as the sign of God's favor. Perhaps, it is also why we count as heroes those who have fought and died for our national freedom, while we are likely to consider the premature deaths of missionaries and their children as tragic wastes.

The idolatrous juggling of God *and* America is not just a problem for nominal Christians. Even insightful and respected Christian leaders are in danger of propagating the false reference point of patriotism by calling us to such things as a "single-minded dedication" to returning America to its rightful "place of strength, stability, and prominence…in an increasingly complicated and competitive global environment."[155] A statement like that should make all sorts of alarms go off inside the heart of the God-first disciple, yet we can easily start to nod our heads in agreement.

To be clear, there is absolutely nothing inherently wrong with paying our taxes, serving our country, or even thanking God for the unique blessings it offers us. Those can be good things. As Christians, however, we need to put to death anything in our lives that sets itself up as being worthy of the "single-minded dedication" that we owe to Jesus Christ alone. He defines us, not our nationality or ethnicity. For in him there is "no Jew, Greek…" Christ is all to us, and thus it is his kingdom, not America's, that we should devote our lives to expanding.

Intellect

On the surface, knowledge itself is the reference point for the intellectual, and education is the key to unlocking humanity's

---

[155] Promotional for *The Seven Faith Tribes* by George Barna, access date May 29, 2012, http://www.barna.org/store?page=shop.product_details&flypage=flypage.tpl&product_id=64&category_id=1&keyword=culture.

potential. Though, as many folks have said before, the more we know, the more we realize we do not know. Combine this disillusioned pursuit of knowledge with the general distrust of absolute realities that pervades our academic circles, and we get an interesting result; presentation becomes more important than substance, and having ideas that are well received is better than having ones that are true.

When clever, new ideas are scarce, we can quickly resort to questioning everything and everyone around us. The more questions we raise, the smarter we appear without ever having to know or stand for anything ourselves. Though the questions may be void of substance themselves, when asked the right way they have the power to cast just enough doubt upon a person or an idea as to undermine. Even obvious truth can be rendered irrelevant in this way. To make matters worse, our questions are rarely meant to lead to answers. The goal is rather to get lost in an open dialogue with people who are diverse and creative and as open-minded as we are.

This is only one of many ways that intellect can become a false reference point. But it is one that is particularly appealing to young Christians who, for various reasons, are tired of doing church the same old way it has always been done. Rather than humbly learning from the two thousand years of accumulated wisdom and experience of the church, our tendency is to throw it all away. The wheel, so to speak, is constantly being reinvented from the ground up. In many cases, Scripture itself is thrown out for messages that are more loving, tolerant, and relevant to the "itching ears" around us and useful for growing our ranks quickly.[156]

It is not that dialogue or questions are bad. After all, Scripture demands that we test everything.[157] However, such godly testing should always be guided by its benefit to the kingdom of God. In other words, we do not argue for argument's sake. Nor do we acquire knowledge to make our name known, but rather to transform us into the image and likeness of our Creator and provide the foundation for fulfilling our common mission of going, baptizing, and teaching.

---

[156] 2 Timothy 4:3–4.

[157] 1 Thessalonians 5:21; 1 John 4:1.

Nature

People have been worshiping creation for a long time. While we may not bow down to a statue of mother earth or father heaven, our subtle Christian twist on this ancient practice is to turn the goal of stewarding creation from spreading God's rule to preserving nature (including ourselves). In nature-first living, labels like organic, recyclable, biodegradable, and green become the markers of godly decision-making, and sanctification becomes a matter of progressive reduction of our carbon footprint.

There is some truth here, as with most false reference points. We do have a responsibility to care for ourselves and creation in a way that maximizes God's glory. Yet we must remember that maximizing God's glory, according to his plan, primarily means multiplying his wholly devoted image-bearers and not preserving our bodies along with the rest of creation. To the degree that something natural or otherwise aids in our ability to make disciples, then we do it. Otherwise, we let it go. To make nature an end in itself is to set it at odds with God-centered stewardship.

Immaturity

There is a stage of life in between childhood and adulthood, where immaturity is not only accepted but praised. For many of us, the lack of responsibility, in combination with adult-like abilities, make these the "best years" of life; often, this is a reference point we look forward to as kids, revel in as young adults, and look back upon fondly as older adults. As secular writer Kay S. Hyowitz notes, young men have a particularly hard time breaking free from this rut of immaturity.

With women moving ahead in our advanced economy, husbands and fathers are now optional, and the qualities of character men once needed to play their roles—fortitude, stoicism, courage, fidelity—are obsolete, even a little embarrassing.

Today's pre-adult male is like an actor in a drama in which he only knows what he shouldn't say. He has to compete in a fierce job market, but he can't act too bossy or self-confident. He should be sensitive but not paternalistic, smart but not cocky. To deepen his predicament, because he is single, his advisers and confidants are generally undomesticated guys just like him.

Relatively affluent, free of family responsibilities, and entertained by an array of media devoted to his every pleasure, the single young man can live in pig heaven—and often does. Women put up with him for a while, but then in fear and disgust either give up on any idea of a husband and kids or just go to a sperm bank and get the DNA without the troublesome man. But these rational choices on the part of women only serve to legitimize men's attachment to the sand box. Why should they grow up? No one needs them anyway. There's nothing they have to do. They might as well just have another beer.[158]

Scripture speaks of such immaturity as being like infants "tossed back and forth by the waves, and blown here and there by every wind of teaching and by the cunning and craftiness of men in their deceitful scheming."[159] Looking around churches these days, it is saddening how prevalent and acceptable such immaturity is, even within marriages. Some of us men have had access to Scripture and sound biblical teaching for five, ten, fifteen years or even more and yet have nothing to show for it. We ought to be teachers by now, but our ambivalence to growth requires a constant rehashing of the "elementary teachings about Christ."[160]

True disciples long for growth. Regardless of society's shifting reference points, they happily answer Scripture's call to ever-increasing maturity,[161] for their eyes are on the kingdom. Wise and

---

[158] Kay S. Hymowitz, "Where Have All the Good Men Gone?" *The Wall Street Journal*, February 19, 2011, http://online.wsj.com/article_email/SB10001424052748704409004576146321725889448-lMyQjAxMTAxMDIwMTEyNDEyWj.html.

[159] Ephesians 4:14.

[160] Hebrews 5:11–6:2.

[161] 1 Corinthians 14:20; 1 Peter 2:2.

godly counsel is invited and heeded, whether it be encouragement or rebuke. For both are welcomed in the pursuit of balanced image bearing, and though structure and expectations may seem strange at first, the disciple embraces them as God given and God modeled.

Food

Gluttony is probably the most obvious form of food idolatry. Traditionally, the "excessive greed for food or drink"[162] was held as one of the seven deadly sins, along with pride, covetousness, lust, anger, envy, and sloth. These sins were called "deadly" because of their fatal effect on spiritual progress.[163] It would seem that we have outgrown such nomenclature, preferring instead to relabel sins like gluttony as psychiatric disorders, such binge eating and bulimia nervosa.

With sin recast as disease, we have done two very important things. First, we have taken ourselves from a position of responsibility to that of a victim of cruel circumstance. Second, we have outsourced our prophetic voice to the health professionals of the world. While Scripture clearly condemns gluttony, we have created a loophole for ourselves to pursue food as an end in itself, a source of comfort in which we can forget about the day's worries for a moment. Meanwhile, God's people are afraid to say anything, lest they ruin our self-image.

Of course, gluttony is not the only way food can distract us. We can run from it as the enemy to our idol of the perfect body image, or we can simply become "foodies" and distract ourselves with the relentless pursuit of palatal perfection. This false reference point is what C. S. Lewis referred to as the "gluttony of delicacy."[164] Whether it be the ideal cappuccino or roll of sushi or microbrew beer, the temptation is to spend vast amounts of the time, energy, and money that God has lent us finding and consuming our choice delicacy rather than investing in eternity.

---

[162] M. H. Manser, *Zondervan Dictionary of Bible Themes* (Grand Rapids, MI: Zondervan, 1999).

[163] *Merriam-Webster's Collegiate Dictionary*, 11th ed. (Springfield, MA: Merriam-Webster, 2003).

[164] C. S. Lewis, *The Screwtape Letters* (New York, NY: HarperCollins, 2001), 88–89.

Food is clearly a necessity for life, and just as clearly, it was created to be enjoyed, not merely consumed.[165] So the problem with gluttony, whether in excess or delicacy, is not that we eat food or even like to eat food. Rather, the problem is that food itself becomes an end goal, or primary reference point for how we spend our time, talent, and treasure. In this case food has become an idol and we must act decisively to put it to death.

Talents

Eventually in our walk through Colossians 3, we will get to verse 17, which reads: "And whatever you do, whether in word or deed, do it all in the name of the Lord Jesus, giving thanks to God the Father through him." Many of us think that this verse means that whatever we are already doing, we ought to do it to the best of our abilities, because when we do something well as Christians, whether it is schoolwork, a sport, a musical instrument, or a job, God inherently gets the glory. Similarly, many of us believe that the way to get him even more glory is to thank him whenever we earn whatever accolades accompany our particular pursuit.

Thus, we work hard at everything we put our hands to, and if we find something we are particularly good at, then we push particularly hard at it. Often that leads to success and accolades. But does this really give God glory? In reality, those who enjoy the most success around us are often those who have the least regard for the things of God. Instead, they build their entire lives—eating, drinking, and sleeping—around training and developing their particular skill. Such singular focus often pays great earthly dividends but brings very little honor and attention to Christ.

---

[165] Why else would God have filled the Garden of Eden with "trees that were pleasing to the eye and good for food" (Genesis 2:9)? Likewise, why would Solomon say, "A man can do nothing better than to eat and drink and find satisfaction in his work. This too, I see, is from the hand of God, for without him, who can eat or find enjoyment" (Ecclesiastes 2:24–25)?

In most cases, we are simply inviting God into *our* dreams and hoping that he will bless our desires for worldly success. Instead of beginning our decisions with the desire to put God first, we are trying to add him onto a mission already in progress. Ironically, the more we get drawn into perfecting our talents "for" him, the more we tend to confuse these natural talents with spiritual gifts and the less time we spend with God. This is not to say that we should avoid developing whatever talents we have been given, but we must not trick ourselves into thinking that Christianity means doing everything the pagans around us do, just better.

We should also beware of passing this talent-first reference point along to our children. For while it is not wrong to desire our kids to succeed emotionally, athletically, academically, and artistically, we have to be cognizant of how these pursuits can add to or distract from our (and their) kingdom-first pursuit. All too often, these *get-to* activities become *have-to* activities—filling up our nights and weekends and pulling us away from opportunities to fellowship with other believers and to be intentionally ministering to unbelievers on Christ's behalf.

American Dream

Of all the false reference points Americans are known for, perhaps the most famous is our shared dream of overcoming whatever circumstances stand in our way to write our own version of "the good life." While unique to a degree, our dreams often share elements like owning a home, having a spouse and 1.86 kids,[166] building nice fences to go around nicely landscaped yards, buying cottages and boats to accompany them, taking frequent vacations, owning multiple cars, and saving up for an early retirement.

These things are not bad or sinful, but they quickly become crippling distractions when we depend on them as the building blocks of a normal life. For in that case, we limit God's hand by assuming that he would never ask us to give one or more of them

---

[166] Average kids per family. 2000 Census of the Unites States of America, http://www.census.gov/population/socdemo/hh-fam/tabST-F1-2000.pdf.

up to further his kingdom. The further we follow our American dream, the harder it gets to fix our eyes on Christ because, as Tozer wrote, "The roots of our hearts have grown into things, and we dare not pull up one rootlet lest we die."[167]

In many ways, retirement is the culmination of the American dream. We work only so long and so hard as to acquire all the pieces of successful living and then we stop. At this point, we tell ourselves that we deserve a rest, and it is time to start truly enjoying life by filling it with seashells, golfing, traveling around the country or the world, and spending time with our grandkids or great grandkids. Retirement tends to be all about us, earned by us and for us.

Certainly, retirement does not have to be so self-focused. We could transform retirement into an opportunity to devote ourselves all the more fully to the work of expanding God's rule through discipleship. That probably will not happen, though, if we do not take some time beforehand to plan accordingly. We need to learn to balance prudent financial planning with rich generosity today, or we will we always opt to hoard wealth for ourselves in the present, while promising to give in the future.

Family and Friends

Here is a reference point that we may never have seriously considered for its idolatrous potential. Indeed, in a Christian climate where we are encouraged to "focus on the family,"[168] we may have difficulty separating duty to family from duty to God, having convinced ourselves that family is the beginning *and* end of our call to ministry. While this family-first focus may answer some of society's ills and aid us in loving our family well, it seems that we have inadvertently set ourselves up to neglect our neighbors most in need of our loving presence.

---

[167] Tozer, *Pursuit*, 22.

[168] To be clear, Focus on the Family Ministries, which I am alluding to here, has done *much* good for promoting the nurturing of our families and children. I do not want to downplay that good, *but* I do want to point out that the missional premise implied in the title is thoroughly flawed and encourages a family-first idolatry that is all too common among professing Christian families today.

Given Scripture's repeated mention of family and our responsibility to them—honor and obey our parents,[169] sacrificially love our wives,[170] respect and submit to our husbands,[171] train up our children through intentional discipleship (without exasperating them),[172] and provide for the needs of our family[173]—it is easy to see why we would gravitate toward them. It can even be argued that Scripture advocates a preferential provision for family.

However, that is not all that Scripture has to say about family. We must balance those passages with others, like the one at the beginning of this chapter where Jesus tells one man to leave his family responsibilities behind and another to make a clean break with his family to follow Jesus. There is also the passage where Jesus says: "If anyone comes to me and does not hate his father and mother, his wife and children, his brothers and sisters—yes, even his own life—he cannot be my disciple."[174]

In reconciling these apparently paradoxical stances, we will quickly realize that Jesus is not calling for an active hate of our family. How could he be, when Scripture commands that we love not only our family but our neighbors and enemies as well? But that does not take away from the severity of Christ's actual call, which is to value his kingdom so far above our own family that our reckless pursuit of him will often look like hateful disregard for our family.[175]

For example, putting God's kingdom first may lead us to take up a life on a foreign mission field when our parents raised us to take over the family business. Similarly, we may find ourselves far from brothers, sisters, nieces, nephews, and cousins, missing all manner of birthday parties, graduations, sporting events, weddings, and even funerals, as we faithfully labor for the multiplication of God's rule.

---

[169] Exodus 20:12; Ephesians 6:2; Colossians 3:2.

[170] Ephesians 5:25–27; Colossians 3:19.

[171] Ephesians 5:22–23, 33; Colossians 3:18.

[172] Deuteronomy 6:4–9; Colossians 3:21.

[173] 1 Timothy 5:8.

[174] Luke 14:26.

[175] Consider Abraham's willingness to sacrifice Isaac (Genesis 22:1–19).

If we have started a family of our own, then we will constantly be tempted to put their desires, comfort, and worldly success in front of the kingdom's advancement. While the two are not always mutually exclusive, they are not always mutually inclusive either. Professing Christians and outright pagans alike will appeal to our sense of parental duty as they urge us toward safer neighborhoods, higher-performing schools (or even homeschooling), and better-paying, more secure jobs. If we buy into such reference points, family will soon become an unassailable excuse for withdrawing from the world and avoiding those neighbors most desperate for help.

For the true believer, the reference point is God's kingdom. It is our highest priority and the one that gives context to everything else, including our families. If we have children, they join in our mission, rather than become it.[176] Though we start expanding God's rule in our own homes, the goal is always to take it "to the ends of the earth."

We do not start aiming for the ends of the earth once our kids are grown; we take them with us today and allow them to join in the process of making disciples from their birth. The safety and educational opportunities of our children are fine things to consider, but these should not keep us from places where God's kingdom is undermanned and underarmed. Indeed, the *right* amount of safety and the *right* kind of education for our kids will only make sense in the context of a kingdom pursuit, where we are measuring our options by how they add or detract from our family's desire and ability to experience and pass on God's rule.

The perfect model for kingdom-focused discipleship is Jesus, whose disciples followed him everywhere. When Jesus walked among the poor and outcast and diseased, so did his disciples. He called them his children, yet he led them to the garden where he was arrested by an armed mob. They were even there at his crucifixion, learning what it meant to lay down everything, including one's life, to take hold of the kingdom of heaven. Most of Jesus's disciples went on themselves to die for the sake of his kingdom. That does not sound like very good earthly parenting, does it?

---

[176] Joshua 24:15.

At the same time, it is important that we not swing too far in the other direction and neglect our families for the sake of our neighbors. This would be the equal and opposite error of neglecting our neighbors for the sake of our children. To avoid either one, we must be constantly reminding ourselves that the two mission fields are not in conflict but designed to be reached simultaneously. Our kids are to be intentionally and particularly poured into *as* we are going about inviting others to experience his love and truth. Neither is the focus, because both are necessary parts of our call to encourage God's rule in those around us.

Religiosity

Although the various forms, rituals, and traditions of Christianity are meant to focus our hearts and minds on worship of our King, they can become themselves false reference points if we are not careful. We can easily go through the motions of church—attending services, praying, singing, tithing, dutifully listening to sermon after sermon, cooking for church potlucks, voting at budget meetings— all without ever giving ourselves wholeheartedly to Jesus and making the multiplication of his rule the great aim of our lives. Driscoll and Breshears describe our predicament in the following terms:

> *In our own day religious people continue in various idolatries when they elevate their denomination, church building, liturgical order, Bible translation, worship style, pastor, theological system, favorite author, or ministry program to where it is a replacement mediator for Jesus, one in which their faith rests to keep close to God. This also explains why any change to the tradition of a religious person is met with such hostility—people cling to their idols, including their church buildings, which are worshiped as sacred, just as the temple was.*

> *Like the Jews in Jesus' day, Christians must be aware of their religious idols. Religious idols include truth, gifts, and morality. These are things that people trust in addition to Jesus Christ for*

their salvation, not unlike the Judaizers who added circumcision
to the gospel and were rebuked by Paul in Galatians as heretics
preaching a false gospel.[177]

Though we be tempted to focus on the particulars of living out
Christianity, in daily life and more formal worship, Christ's
principle of taking our eyes off of life's details to fix them on his
kingdom holds just as true for our religious practices as it does
for our nonreligious ones. Such singular pursuit of Christ's all-
encompassing rule not only bears fruit in our own lives but it gives
God's people a common reference point that we can encourage
each other toward, rather than waging wars among ourselves over
varying methods and styles of worship and ministry.

It will be helpful to keep the idea of religious distractions in
mind as we move forward and examine the various characteristics of
Christ. For each aspect of his character has the potential to become a
false reference point, or god, in itself. And while focusing our lives
on one aspect of godliness may look exceedingly good to others
and to ourselves, our image-bearing capacity will be crippled and,
quite possibly, our lives lost as well. The solution to our tendency
for imbalance is to go all in, from the start. Just as we are to put to
death *all* of our earthly nature, so too are we to put on *all* of Christ.

Anything or Nothing at All

Whether our individual false reference points were addressed in
this list is not particularly important. What is important, however,
is that we realize just how commonplace these deadly idols are in
our lives. In his book *The Screwtape Letters*, C. S. Lewis writes about
the utility of everyday idols from the perspective of one demon
counseling another in the finer points of distraction.

You will say that these are very small sins; and doubtless, like
all young tempters, you are anxious to report some spectacular

---

[177] *Doctrine*, 357–358.

wickedness. But do remember, the only thing that matters is the extent to which you separate the man from the Enemy {God}. It does not matter how small the sins are provided that their cumulative effect is to edge the man away from the Light and out into the Nothing. Murder is no better than cards if cards can do the trick. Indeed the safest road to Hell is the gradual one— the gentle slope, soft underfoot, without sudden turnings, without milestones, without signposts.[178]

Whether it is hideous sin or innocent-appearing religiosity, through the grace and power of the Spirit of God within us, we must put our distraction to death. And we must repeat this process as often as necessary to empty ourselves of ourselves and make room for Christ.

Let us take a minute to prayerfully consider our own lives before moving on. Remember, the specific outcomes of our choices are not nearly as important as the reason behind them. Think about how you spend your time, talent, and treasure. What are you doing with them? Where do they go? What are you building toward? Why? Is it for Jesus's sake, or are your eyes fixed on a false reference point?

---

[178] p. 60–61.

8

Disunity in the Body

But now you must rid yourselves of all such things as these: anger, rage, malice, slander, and filthy language from your lips. Do not lie to each other, since you have taken off your old self with its practices.

—COLOSSIANS 3:8–9

Having examined what it looks like to be distracted by sex, money, and a great deal of other evil desires, let us turn our attention to how using false reference points, no matter what they are, reveals itself in the life of a community of professing believers. Toward this end, let us take up the second list of old-self attributes given by Paul in Colossians 3, seen above in verses 8–9.

While these things—anger, rage, malice, slander, and filthy (or "abusive"[179]) speech—are wrong in themselves, they function more

---

[179] Though at first glance the word for "filthy" language could be taken in many ways, such as swearing or impure talk, the Greek word (aischrologia) is most literally translated as abusive speech. Thus, here in Colossians 3:8, filthy language closely parallels the idea of slander. See R. L. Thomas, *New*

as symptoms of a disease rather than the disease itself. The real disease is that of a self-centered heart, which chases after any and every distraction it sees fit to chase after. This would not be such a huge problem if we were to all live in isolation. However, a life of godliness in the kingdom of heaven assumes community. For there can be no love for others when there are no others around to love.

Even as our desire to flee from worldly distractions tempts us to withdraw from the world, God demands that we be in the world, though not of it, living as salt and light.[180] He demands all the more that we be in regular community with other believers. For we are interdependent members of one body, each relying on the whole for our existence and the fulfillment of our calling.[181]

Each relationship, whether with a believer or an unbeliever, is an opportunity to build, either for the kingdom of heaven or the kingdom of darkness. We build the former by pursuing unity in Jesus Christ and letting his sacrificial love for others flow through our words and deeds. We build the latter simply by accepting the status quo, floating along on the current of a self-centered world ethos. In his letter to the Galatians, Paul contrasts these two mindsets:

> *You, my brothers, were called to be free. But do not use your freedom to indulge the sinful nature; rather, serve one another in love. The entire law is summed up in a single command: "Love your neighbor as yourself." If you keep on biting and devouring each other, watch out or you will be destroyed by each other.*

> —GALATIANS 5:13–15

While we are probably familiar with this notion of "loving our neighbor as ourselves" how many of us have ever wrestled with the practical implications? If we do, then it will not take long before

---

American Standard Hebrew-Aramaic and Greek Dictionaries updated ed. (Anaheim, CA: Foundation, 1998).

[180] Matthew 5: 13–16; John 17:14–18; Hebrews 11:13–16.

[181] 1 Corinthians 12:12–26.

we realize just how hard and all-encompassing such a command can be.

For example, when a neighbor's car breaks down and he risks losing his job because he cannot afford to fix it, would we let him borrow our car or give him the money we had wisely stored away in an emergency account to repair it? Do we ensure that our sick neighbor gets the care and attention that we would demand for ourselves? Do we provide homes and loving families for the fatherless and orphans, the way we do ourselves?

Taking it one step further, what would it look like to "consider others *better* than ourselves," following the example of our King who "made himself nothing, taking the very nature of a servant,"[182] to usher in redemption from sins and a re-created kingdom? Would we give that neighbor with the broken-down car our own new one? Would we sacrifice a certain standard of medical attention or house to ensure that others can have them?

Compare the requisite others-centeredness of God's people to, perhaps, a more familiar reference point: the opening line of the United States Declaration of Independence.

We hold these truths to be self-evident, that all men are created equal, that they are endowed by their Creator with certain unalienable Rights, that among these are Life, Liberty and the Pursuit of Happiness.

In Scripture, love goes to God first and then to others and finally to ourselves. Yet, as typified by our American creed,[183] the priorities in our fallen world run backward, starting with ourselves. God and others are loved only when it is convenient to our lives and the pursuit of our happiness and whatever other reference points we

---

[182] Excerpts taken from Philippians 2:3–7.

[183] Though I use the Declaration of Independence as an example of legitimized and systemic self-love, this disease is not unique to Americans. Sin is no respecter of geographical, social, or economic boundaries. Children are sold into slavery and brothels in Vietnam and Thailand. Towns and villages are ransacked, men and boys tortured and killed, women and girls raped and killed in Sudan and the Congo. Billionaires in India sit idly by while millions starve in their own country, just like we do.

think will lead us there. When other people stand between our unalienable rights and us, then things invariably get ugly. As the apostle James warns, our stilted self-love has a tendency to come out sideways:

> *What causes fights and quarrels among you? Don't they come from your desires that battle within you? You want something but don't get it. You kill and covet, but you cannot have what you want. You quarrel and fight. You do not have, because you do not ask God. When you ask, you do not receive, because you ask with wrong motives, that you may spend what you get on your pleasures.*
>
> —JAMES 4:1–3

Coveting, fighting, and quarreling are the invariable result of self-centered people living in proximity. This is James's argument, and it is also Paul's both to the Galatians, whose self-love has them in danger of "biting and devouring each other," and to the Colossians, whose old selves are wrapped up in anger, rage, malice, slander, and abusive language. Because God's people are expected to live in proximity with both the world and, even more so, with each other, we can expect there to be the potential for a similar level of anger, frustration, and infighting among us.

I encourage you to reflect on your own life for a minute. Where does your self-love lead? How do you react when someone stands in your way? How might you retrain yourself in godliness? Below are a few questions to get you started.

- *Am I easily angered?* What happens, for instance, when I am cut off in traffic or a referee makes a bad call against my favorite sports team? How about when my child draws all over the wall with lipstick or a roommate leaves dishes in the sink? What is my reaction when someone questions my ideas or mocks me?

- *Am I easily enraged?* Does my anger ever become violent and uncontrolled? Do I physically lash out when I lose my temper? Do my family and friends tread lightly around me for fear of setting me off? Do I lash out with words? Are there things that lower my threshold for blowing up, like alcohol?

- *Do I nurture bitterness?* Is there anyone I refuse to forgive? Am I holding onto anger against an individual or a people group? Do I have anyone I would call an enemy? Did a parent, spouse, or close friend ever hurt me? What did I do with that anger? Do I have a coworker or fellow church member whom I refuse to talk to?

- *Am I cynical?*[184] Do I pride myself on being *realistic*? Would others describe my humor as dry or sarcastic? When was the last time anyone asked me why I was so full of hope?

- *Do I justify my anger?* Is my anger different from everybody else's? Do I prefer the term "righteous indignation" to describe my feelings?[185]

- *Am I malicious?* Is there anyone I would love to see fail? Do I attack others with whom I disagree, either openly or in hiding? Do I seek to harm others? Do I sabotage them, actively or by withholding my support?

- *Do I slander others or abuse them with my words?* Do I tear down others with lies or one-sided stories that cast them in dubious light? Do I ask questions meant only to place doubt on the intentions of others? Am I malignant, always complaining about authority and turning folks against each other? Am

---

[184] While we often celebrate cynicism as witty and clever, it can be a sign of a disillusioned heart, smoldering in anger.

[185] Our culture will tell us that we have a right to be angry when others wrong us or stand in the way of us living life to the full. But God says to leave vengeance to him and to love our enemy and forgive him, without regard for circumstance (Matthew 5:39; Deuteronomy 32:35; Romans 12:19).

I quick to criticize other's ideas or actions? Do others not open up to me because they are afraid of me?

While the world tells us to make our own way and pursue whatever we think will make us happy, Jesus expects us to forget about ourselves and focus on him and his righteousness. When it comes to relationships with unbelievers and believers alike, God's righteousness means loving our neighbor as we love ourselves.[186] The tighter we cling to our various false reference points, the more inconvenient and threatening others will seem to us.

Anyone who has spent time in a church can testify to the fact that self-love is as much a problem among professing believers as it is for the world around us. We, too, are sinners stuck in our self-serving ruts and will, despite our best efforts, continue to sin against one another. As we live and work and worship together, differences will come up. Feelings will get hurt. Toes will get stepped on. Sometimes the sharpening from one another will feel more like grating, and often, rebukes will not be offered in gentleness.

Though we must all agree on the number-one priority in life, we will disagree on just about everything else. We will disagree on the type of music to sing during worship services or whether to have music at all. We will disagree on how to go about discipleship and what color carpet to get and whether we sit in pews or chairs and the most effective way to reach out to our hurting world and how best to follow up with new faces.

When we ought to be cheering one another on, the temptation will be to adopt a spirit of ill will toward those who disagree with us on the details. The jealousy and envy of our old self quickly leads to malice, and it is easy, when there are differences, to attack those we are at odds with. In most churches, anger probably rarely builds to the point of a fistfight or even open verbal bashings. Yet

---

[186] Scripture is not telling us, as some will no doubt argue, to first learn how to love ourselves so that we can love others. Rather, Scripture assumes self-love and mentions it only to give sacrificial love context in a world where it is foreign.

our destructive hearts will nevertheless reveal themselves in private gossip held behind the backs of those we disagree with.

Instead of approaching believers whom we have concerns about, we much prefer to sit back and dismantle their character with innocent-sounding statements like, "Can you believe Jackie wanted to do this?" or "If only Tom would see the light, his ministry would really take off." Because the other person is not available for comment, assumptions are made, usually for the worst, and judgment is cast based on our speculations. Is this not the kind of biting and devouring that Paul warns the Galatians against?

Let us not exchange eternity with the King for a life of frustration and aggravation spent jealously defending our rights to earthly life, liberty, and happiness. Instead, let us turn away from ourselves, looking first to King Jesus and letting his loving rule be our reference point. Let us hold fast to his example as we answer his call to consider others more worthy than ourselves. In self-forgetfulness alone will we find freedom to love others as Christ did—unfettered by the conceit that leads to anger, malice, slander, and abusive speech.[187]

---

[187] In contrast to the anger, rage, malice, slander, and abusive speech of the old self stands the bearing with and forgiving of the new self, which leads to unity. Because these characteristics of the new self in Christ are discussed at length in chapters fourteen and fifteen, I will forgo examining them here.

9

Hiding under a Bowl

You are the light of the world. A city on a hill cannot be hidden.
Neither do people light a lamp and put it under a bowl. Instead
they put it on its stand, and it gives light to everyone in the house.
In the same way, let your light shine before men, that they may see
your good deeds and praise your Father in heaven.

—MATTHEW 5:14–16

Though Scripture teaches us about the glorious reward of a singular pursuit of God and the equally horrible suffering that false reference points lead to, it is hard for us to believe in that reality in such a way that it truly changes our lives. The distractions seem too natural and too harmless for us to go about killing any of them.

So life goes on. We remain stuck in the ruts of the world—thinking and acting and living, just like the unbelievers around us. Our lives are as darkness to darkness, thus invalidating any claim we make to know the "true light that gives light to every man."[188] As Jim Elliot, missionary and martyr, put it:

We are so utterly ordinary, so commonplace, while we profess to know a Power, the Twentieth Century does not reckon with. But we are "harmless," and therefore unharmed. We are pacifists, non-militants, conscientious objectors in this battle-to-the-death with principalities and powers in high places....The world cannot hate us, we are too much like its own. Oh that God would make us dangerous![189]

The same distractions that lead to infighting among professing Christians lead to a certain level of peace between professing Christians and the world. For, as Elliot pointed out, when we adopt the world's standards, it cannot hate us or war against us.

Pacifism with the world did not used to be an option for professing Christians. In Jesus's day, and for several centuries thereafter, aligning yourself with him was seen as a clear departure from societal and religious norms, and it came with persecution.[190] Even when persecution was absent, the cost was not. Jesus would simply not allow folks to come to him still clinging to their worldly idols.[191] The choice was always him or the world, the kingdom of light or the kingdom of darkness.

When Constantine ended the public persecution of Christians in the Roman Empire, much of that changed.[192] Widespread persecution ended, and professing believers no longer had earth dwellers telling them that they could not have the world if they wanted Christ. At the same time, there were not enough folks in the church

---

[188] John 1:8.

[189] Elisabeth Elliot, *Shadow of the Almighty* (New York, NY: HarperCollins, 1979), 79.

[190] John 12:43.

[191] Luke 18:18–23.

[192] Several years after becoming the first Christian emperor of Rome, Constantine I issued the Edict of Milan in 313 AD, which officially ended the public persecution of Christians.

willing to remind professing believers that they could not have Christ if they wanted to chase after the things of this world, too.

Over the centuries this lack of persecution from without and prophetic voice from within has led to increasing numbers of false reference points becoming acceptable add-ons to the professing Christian's pursuit of God.[193] Thus, in many situations today we find ourselves as a community of professing believers sitting in the same boat as the world. To tell the world of its idolatry would force us to reckon with our own (e.g., security, career, and family). So, we say and do nothing and trust that everyone else will, too—leaving no one to expose our sham of a faith.

Let us consider one example from our nation's history of how professing believers have chosen, repeatedly over many years, to hide the light of Christ. Though this is not the only area where we have sacrificed our prophetic voice, our pacifism in this battle is worth considering because it has been so costly historically, and continues to be so in our day as we propagate the sinful and unjust systems passed down to us by our ancestors. The example I would like to consider is that of slavery and racism in America.

For much of our nation's early history, most church leaders either supported slavery outright or neatly sidestepped the issue with silence. Despite its gross injustices and inherent violence, slavery was largely ignored by the affluent white church, much the way the priest and Levite walked right past the battered man in Jesus's parable of the Good Samaritan. With so many church members benefiting directly and indirectly from human trafficking, is it easy to see how the false reference points of comfort and security led so many leaders to say so little against the injustices of slavery.

After the Civil War, things should have gotten better, right? In some ways they probably did, but in many other ways, the oppression merely changed forms. Those with resources in the church sat by while black men and women were dumped into an

---

[193] I use "prophetic" here in the sense of being a truth teller who corrects moral and religious abuses on God's behalf. All Christians are called to take on this role, using the truth God has already revealed. In contrast, the *gift* of prophecy entails bringing new revelations from God to his people.

under-resourced cycle with no money or education upon which to build a life. Reparations were either absent or woefully inadequate. Slaves were no longer bought and sold, but inequalities continued to be passed from generation to generation due to the lack of opportunities available to the under-resourced.

Speaking in very general terms, blacks have been stuck in that under-resourced cycle ever since, while whites, again in very general terms, have been operating in an independent and well-resourced cycle. While the affluent (and largely white) church's considerable political and social influence could have been leveraged to bring about justice on a large scale, we were afraid to rock the boat. Crossing over from the resourced cycle to the under-resourced one remained too costly to our false reference points of comfort and security, so we sat by and watched.

John Perkins, founder of the Christian Community Development Association, was born in rural Mississippi in 1930 and got to experience firsthand the apathy of the affluent white church. As he puts it:

I did not see white Christianity as meaningful either. To me it was part of that whole system that helped dehumanize and destroy black people; that system which identified me as a nigger. So how could the white church really be concerned about me?

I had lived in the South. I had drunk at separate drinking fountains. I had ridden in the back of buses. And never in the South had I heard one white Christian speak out against the way whites treated blacks as second-class citizens.

I had never accepted that falsehood that I was a second-class citizen. Nor had I ever accepted the myth that I was a nigger. So I did not see the white church as relevant to me and my needs.[194]

---

[194] *Let Justice Roll Down* (Ventura, CA: Regal, 1976), 57.

White churches across America waffled on Scripture's manifold call to justice. In doing so, they abdicated their prophetic voice during a pivotal time in America's history. While the unity of blacks and whites in Christ would have been a powerful testimony to the transcendent nature of God's kingdom in such decisive time, Christians of both colors instead chose to sit on the sidelines waiting for the activist and fanatic to show us what morality looked like. Here is how Perkins describes it:

> I went to many civil rights rallies and talked with a lot of the people. I was an evangelical Christian, and our Voice of Calvary Bible Institute was growing. Our young people in Bible school and college were gaining a political and economic awareness, and a spiritual awareness.

> But going to those political meetings I could feel in my bones there was going to be trouble. Rioting and burning and trouble. Why? Because issues were being raised. Valid issues. But they were being raised in and by groups that were not primarily evangelical.

> The contribution of the civil rights movement to the black man's struggle for justice and equality is one that is undeniably great. And this is so, because those who led the movement were committed men and women. They were committed to the cause. And to the struggle.

> But how sad that so few individuals equally committed to Jesus Christ ever became a part of that movement. For what all the political activity needed—and lacked—was spiritual input. Even now, I do not understand why so many evangelicals find a sense of commitment to civil rights and to Jesus Christ an "either-or" proposition.

> One of the great tragedies of the civil rights movement is that evangelicals surrendered their leadership in the movement by default to those with either a bankrupt theology or no theology at all, simply because the vast majority of Bible-believing Christians

ignored a great and crucial opportunity in history for genuine
ethical action. The evangelical church—whose basic theology is
the same as mine—had not gone on to preach the whole gospel.

So I decided to act, and this placed me squarely between two camps.
I knew, of course, that we wouldn't get anywhere unless we started
with the gospel that calls men to Christ for forgiveness and God's
strength. For man cannot create justice by human manipulation
alone. But, at the same time, the church, by so-called "spiritual"
manipulation alone, cannot effect justice.[195]

Sadly, it was not until public opinion began to shift that white
evangelicals, whose lives continued to be wrapped up in the affluent
culture, joined en masse the call for racial equality. By now most
of us who come from affluent, middle- or upper-class backgrounds,
probably assume that systemic justice has already been achieved.
This assumption leads us to believe that *if* any inequalities do still
exist, they arise entirely from the individual's lack of initiative or
the deplorable choice to accept such noncompetitive practices as
"single-parent homes, having too many children, not stressing
education, being too willing to receive welfare, and being unable
to move beyond the past."[196]

Affluent folks think such things, in part, because we want desperately to move forward. Until we let go of the past, we tell ourselves, there will be no future. I think that if we are honest, though,
we also say these things because we want no part of our brother's
burden. It is his, after all, and he should have to make his own way,
the same way we have made ours.

Of course, the preoccupation with individual responsibility ignores the slant in the playing field that favors the already
resourced. As authors and professors Michael O. Emerson and
Christian Smith write:

---

[195] Perkins, *Justice*, 103.

[196] Michael O. Emerson and Christian Smith, *Divided By Faith* (New York, NY: Oxford University Press, 2000), 109.

This {individualistic} perspective misses that white Americans are far more likely than black Americans to get a solid education, avoid being a victim of a crime, and have family and friends with money to help when extra cash is needed for college, a car, or a house. This perspective misses that white Americans are far more likely to have networks and connections that lead to good jobs than are black Americans. This perspective misses that white Americans are more likely to get fair treatment in the court system than are African Americans....{Moreover,} the individualistic perspective encourages people to dismiss such evidence as liberal, wrongheaded, overblown, or as isolated incidents.[197]

Despite all our advances, injustice continues to plague the under-resourced and voiceless minorities in our country. It does not matter that we did not start the process. The reality is, it exists and we perpetuate it—not with any active participation, but simply by going about life as usual. The inertia of society's status quo keeps two cycles spinning and spinning at a safe distance from each other.

Those with opportunities and education and wealth generate more of those things and pass them onto their children and avoid those without, lest they forfeit their place among the resourced. And those without opportunities and education and wealth pass along that legacy of instability to their children, which often cripples their ability to receive and grow in the gospel.

Affluent churches could speak up on this issue, but usually they do not. Perhaps we are afraid of the implications, knowing that to demand anything more of our members than cross-cultural friendships would expose the depth of our greed and our idolatrous fixation on comfort and safety. Whatever the reason, our pacifism will give way to our death. For when we ought to be making war on our evil desires, we find excuses not to, and sin is left unopposed to ravage our souls.

---

[197] Emerson and Smith, *Divided*, 90.

At the end of part three, we will look again at the call to unity in the body of Christ and what that might look like for us today. For now, though, it may be helpful to take a minute to consider the ways that you and I have unwittingly adopted the false reference points around us. Think not only of the comfort and security that cause us to withdraw from issues of injustice, but think back through the rest of part two as well. What false reference points stood out for you? How have you built your life around them? How does that affect your desire to call other Christians to holiness and non-Christians to their very great reward in Christ? Are you and I hiding under a bowl, or is Christ's light shining forth through us?

III
Putting on Christ

Therefore, as God's chosen people, holy and dearly loved, clothe yourselves with compassion, kindness, humility, gentleness and patience. Bear with each other and forgive whatever grievances you may have against one another. Forgive as the Lord forgave you. And over all these virtues put on love, which binds them all together in perfect unity. Let the peace of Christ rule in your hearts, since as members of one body you were called to peace. And be thankful.

—COLOSSIANS 3:12–15

10

Love

And over all these virtues put on love, which binds them all together in perfect unity.

—COLOSSIANS 3:14

L et us begin our journey through the image of our Creator (i.e., Christlikeness or righteousness) with the virtue of love, rather than end with it, as Paul does. You see, Scripture has a lot to say about love—far too much to try to cover in one chapter, or even one book for that matter. Yet at the same time, love is not its own virtue, so much as a synopsis of the various attributes of godliness that make up our default calling as believers. As Paul wrote to the Corinthians:

Love is patient, love is kind. It does not envy, it does not boast, it is not proud. It is not rude, it is not self-seeking, it is not easily angered, it keeps no record of wrongs. Love does not delight in evil but rejoices with the truth. It always protects, always trusts, always hopes, always perseveres.

—1 CORINTHIANS 13:4–7

Likewise, Jesus taught that the hundreds of commands in Scripture can all be summed up in the two commands to love God and love others.[198]

> *"Love the Lord your God with all your heart and with all your soul and with all your mind." This is the first and greatest commandment. And the second is like it: "Love your neighbor as yourself." All the Law and the Prophets hang on these two commandments.*

> —MATTHEW 22:37–40

Jesus was not offering something new to replace something old when he said this, for he was quoting two of the oldest commandments given to God's people.[199] Rather, he was reminding his followers that the purpose behind the law and the prophets (i.e., God's will of desire) and even other virtues is to teach us what it looks like to love God and others. It is through the law, prophets, and other virtues that love finds its form and definition.

Because of the premium Scripture places on love, we can be tempted to focus solely on it and forget all about the commands and virtues that underlie it. Without them, however, love turns into a nebulous and subjective idea without hope of consistent and fruitful application. By considering love at the beginning, we will see how the subsequent virtues are the natural and tangible result of a heart that is wholly devoted to King Jesus.

When Paul speaks of love in Colossians 3:14 he is speaking almost exclusively about the command to love others. However, from other parts of Scripture, we know that the commands—to love God and to love others—are inseparable. That is, we cannot love others without first loving God. For, "This is how we know that we love the children of God: by loving God and carrying out his commands."[200] Nor can

---

[198] Matthew 22:37–40; Romans 13:8–10; Galatians 5:614, 22.

[199] Deuteronomy 6:5; Leviticus 19:18.

[200] 1 John 5:2.

we love God without also loving others. As the apostle John writes, "If anyone says, 'I love God,' yet hates his brother, he is a liar."[201]

Given the inseparable nature of the two commands for love, it is important to address both. Let us start by considering the all-of-life-encompassing love for God. This is the first and greatest commandment from which everything flows, including our love for others.[202] Afterward we will examine the command to love others. This second discussion is intentionally brief and may feel inadequate. Please allow the subsequent chapters and virtues to fill in the gaps as best they can.

Love for God

"Love the Lord your God with all your heart and with all your soul and with all your mind." Though the quote is not word for word, Jesus undoubtedly draws this first commandment from the same passage in Deuteronomy that we examined in connection with our common calling to multiply God's rule. Here it is again:

> *Hear, O Israel: The Lord our God, the Lord is one. Love the Lord your God with all your heart and with all your soul and with all your strength. These commandments that I give you today are to be upon your hearts. Impress them on your children. Talk about them when you sit at home and when you walk along the road, when you lie down and when you get up. Tie them as symbols on your hands and bind them on your foreheads. Write them on the doorframes of your houses and on your gates.*
>
> —DEUTERONOMY 6:4–9

Let us think about two observations from the text. First, notice how the command to love God relates to the overall subject of the passage, which is submission to and multiplication of his kingdom

---

[201] 1 John 4:20.

[202] As we saw in part one, the call to a singular love of God, which observes and passes on singular obedience to him, is nothing more than a restatement of the commandment to seek first God's kingdom and his righteousness.

rule. It is through observing and passing on all the "commands, decrees, and laws" the Lord has given that his people demonstrate their singular love for him. Jesus makes the same connection between doing his will and loving him when he said, "If you love me, you will obey what I command."[203] Again the connection is confirmed by the words of the apostle John, who wrote, "This is love for God: to obey his commands."[204]

The second observation for us to consider is the all-of-life-encompassing nature of the command to love God. The specific elements in the lists—heart, soul, and strength in Deuteronomy, and heart, soul, and mind in Matthew—are not nearly so important individually as they are collectively, emphasizing the completeness of the believer's desire. As we saw in creation, life cannot be divided into secular and religious, for Christ is all and in all. The singular passion for him directs the believer's every emotion, thought, and effort, no matter the circumstance or setting.

Only when our lives have been emptied of everything else can we say with any confidence that Christ is all in our hearts and our souls and our minds. The details of life—where we live, work, and study, what we eat and wear, how we spend our time and money—must be cast down before Jesus can be all. We must approach him without dreams, agendas, skill sets, or preferences, focused entirely on seeing his kingdom expand as we take on his righteous rule and teach others to do the same.

Such thorough emptying requires a deep and tangible delight in God. While such is the mindset of all God's people, for illustration's sake, let us reflect on the example of one man, David Brainerd, an eighteenth-century missionary to the Native Americans. Though he was not a particularly successful missionary with regard to numbers of converts, and though he spent only a short time here on earth, his singular passion for Christ was unmistakable and left an indelible mark on God's people. Below is an excerpt from his

---

[203] John 14:15.
[204] 1 John 5:3.

diary, written at one of the low points in his long struggle against tuberculosis, which eventually claimed his life.

In the evening also I found the consolations of God were not small: I was then willing to live, and in some respects desirous of it, that I might do something for the dear kingdom of Christ; and yet death appeared pleasant: so that I was in some measure in a strait between two, having a desire to depart. I am often weary of this world, and want to leave it on that account; but it is desirable to be drawn, rather than driven, out of it.[205]

Notice Brainerd's focus. While most of us would have been distracted with self-pity, his thoughts were fixed on God. He had emptied himself of everything until all that remained was his love for "the dear kingdom of Christ." And what delight he found in his King!

Longed to spend the little inch of time I have in the world more for God. Felt a spirit of seriousness, tenderness, sweetness, and devotion; and wished to spend the whole night in prayer and communion with God.[206]

By the world's standards, Brainerd's life was wasted. It ended early, as the lives of the faithful often do. His death at the age of twenty-nine was undoubtedly hastened by the stubbornness with which Brainerd continued to minister even after days with little food, cold nights spent without shelter, and prolonged episodes of coughing up blood.

By the kingdom's standards, however, Brainerd's was a glorious life. Just as a falling star bears light only as it is consumed by its journey through a foreign atmosphere, so his earthly sojourn was set ablaze by his otherworldly love for God. His diary reminds us of what it means to joyfully give up everything for a place in the

---

[205] Entry on June 22, 1745. David Brainerd and Jonathan Edwards (editor), *The Life and Diary of David Brainerd* (Peabody, MA: Hendrickson, 2006), 169.

[206] Entry on July 18, 1745. Brainerd and Edwards, *Diary*, 170.

kingdom with the King. "Oh how sweet it is," Brainerd wrote, "to be spent and worn out for God!"[207]

Love for Neighbors

"Love your neighbor as yourself" is the second of the two commands through which Jesus says the rest of Scripture finds its fulfillment.[208] It is inseparable from the first: to love God with a singular and preeminent love. You see, as we fix our hearts and minds on King Jesus, we are transformed into the image of Love himself. Our lives then become a continual retelling, in word and deed, of our Creator's tender compassion for his rebellious creatures. As the apostle John puts it:

> *This is how we know what love is: Jesus Christ laid down his life for us. And we ought to lay down our lives for our brothers. If anyone has material possessions and sees his brother in need but has no pity on him, how can the love of God be in him? Dear children, let us not love with words or tongue but with actions and in truth.*

> *— 1 JOHN 3:16–18*

Compassion realized at any cost—that is how Scripture defines love for others. We are to remember how Jesus, who had no sin, died a horrible and painful death for our sins. Then, we are to go and do likewise. John gives us no time to stall with speculation regarding the practical application of Jesus's sacrifice; laying down our lives for our brothers and sisters means showing them pity regardless of the cost to ourselves.

---

[207] Entry on February 21, 1746. Brainerd and Edwards, *Diary*, 186.

[208] We do not love others because they are lovable, or deserving of love, because none of us are. No matter how good we appear, we are hopelessly wretched and sinful. I mention this because in our efforts to be more loving, we are prone to want to boost others' self-esteem, rather than their esteem of Christ. The purpose of love for others is meant to show them the love of Christ, not their own deservingness of love, lest we inspire a dead-end entitlement to love by feeding into a person's earthly self-love.

No alternative for the true believer is offered. Pity your brother and sister for their common human spiritual depravity. Love them by inviting them quickly and frequently to know Christ. Pity also their physical needs. Be generous rather than comfortable, and right injustices rather than hide in safety.

Looking again to Brainerd's example, we can see this twofold pity for spiritual and physical brokenness lived out. His Christlike compassion for lost souls is what first led him to bring the gospel to the Native Americans. It also sustained him as he faithfully preached for years, despite his constantly ailing health and the lack of any perceivable spiritual headway. During that time, Brainerd lived among the Native Americans and learned to pity their physical struggles as well, including the lack of available education. His diary is littered with references to aid for such needs.

Like Jesus's love for us, Brainerd's love for his neighbor extended far beyond the worldly default of being kind only to those who were kind to him. Instead of being satisfied with loving his brothers and sisters and friends, he sought out an audience of strangers who, more often than not, rejected him and spat on his most earnest offers of God's love. While Brainerd was certainly disheartened at times, his faithful one-directional love was exactly the type of love that Jesus commended to his disciples:

But I tell you who hear me: Love your enemies, do good to those who hate you, bless those who curse you, pray for those who mistreat you. If someone strikes you on one cheek, turn to him the other also. If someone takes your cloak, do not stop him from taking your tunic. Give to everyone who asks you, and if anyone takes what belongs to you, do not demand it back. Do to others as you would have them do to you.

If you love those who love you, what credit is that to you? Even "sinners" love those who love them. And if you do good to those who are good to you, what credit is that to you? Even "sinners" do that. And if you lend to those from whom you expect repayment, what credit is that to you? Even "sinners" lend to "sinners," expecting to be repaid in full. But love your enemies, do good to them, and lend to them without expecting to get anything back. Then your reward will be great, and you will be sons of the Most High, because he is kind to the ungrateful and wicked.

—LUKE 6:27–35

Godly love extends beyond the body of Christ. It seeks out those who would hurt it, and when hurt, it continues on, exposing itself again to the violence of its enemies. Forceful demands are met and exceeded. With all sense of personal rights discarded to make more room for Jesus, it is nothing to give freely of time, talent, and treasure with no expectation of anything in return. Instead of holding grudges, godly love drives the believer into earnest prayer and service on behalf of their enemies.

All that may sound a little too strange and a little too extreme. Our earthly nature bucks against the otherworldliness of Christ, pleading for some sort of compromise with the status quo—perhaps an acceptance of what pastor and author Dietrich Bonhoeffer saw as the false Protestant ethic "which diluted Christian love into patriotism, loyalty to friends, and industriousness."[209] Yet, despite the temptation from both within and outside of our church walls, the extraordinary cannot be merged with ordinary. If it does, we become as lightless lamps and saltless salt, without a place in the kingdom of heaven.

Much more could be said about love. However, this is enough upon which to start. Let us continue on to the rest of Christ's virtues that we, as his followers and image bearers, are called to put on and that together define this notion of Christlike love.

---

[209] Bonhoeffer, *Discipleship*, 152–153.

11

Compassion (and Kindness)[210]

Therefore, as God's chosen people, holy and dearly loved, clothe yourselves with compassion, kindness...

—COLOSSIANS 3:12

Our God is a compassionate God, and he desires to be known as such. We see this in the way God announced himself to Moses as he passed in front of him on Mount Sinai saying, "The Lord, the Lord, the compassionate and gracious God, slow to anger, abounding in love and faithfulness."[211] Moreover, the mercy and compassion of God are frequently mentioned in Scripture as both a cause for praising God[212] and as the only basis for appeals to him made by his fallen creatures.[213]

As God's chosen people, we are to clothe ourselves with his compassion. It is how we reintroduce the world to its Creator,

---

[210] Compassion and kindness overlap quite a bit, so we will forgo a specific discussion of kindness. The main difference is that, unlike compassion, kindness does not flow from pity so much as from goodness and integrity of heart.

[211] Exodus 34:6.

[212] Nehemiah 9:17, 31; Psalm 78:38; 103:8; 111:4; 116:5; Lamentations 3:22; Joel 2:13; James 5:11.

[213] Psalm 25:6; 51:1; 69:19; Daniel 9:18.

shining forth his heavenly image for all to see, hear, and feel. Here we must be careful to maintain the distinction between Godlike compassion and compassion according to any other standard, for even compassion can be turned into a false reference point when we choose to live it out according to our terms.

The distinction between Godlike, or Christlike, compassion and other forms is not an issue of definition, for the dictionary definition—"sympathetic consciousness of others' distress together with a desire to alleviate it"[214]—will serve us quite well. Nor does our problem arise because we think compassion unimportant or the needs in our world underwhelming. Instead, the distinction arises when we try to decide which kind of distress—physical or spiritual—is most worth alleviating.[215]

Sadly, we jump right into dividing and prioritizing without much consideration for whether the dichotomy between physical and spiritual is helpful to the kingdom or consistent with the story of God in Scripture. The inevitable result is a crippling imbalance in our image bearing, which we will examine shortly.

Before we look our tendencies toward *imbalance*, however, it is worth taking a brief look at the *balance* of Jesus, in whose likeness we are to be transformed. Remember the words of the Apostle John:

This how we know what love is: Jesus Christ laid down his life for us. And we ought to lay down our lives for our brothers. If anyone has material possessions and sees his brother in need but has no pity on him, how can the love of God be in him? Dear children, let us not love with words or tongue but with actions and in truth.

—1 JOHN 3:16–18

---

[214] http://www.merriam-webster.com/dictionary/compassion, access date May 30, 2012.

[215] The fact that we prioritize between physical and spiritual needs does not mean that we do not value both on some level, but that meeting one is given clear precedence over meeting the other.

The compassion that Paul describes in Colossians is the same tender, active pity that John describes in the passage above.[216] It is worth noting, again, the inescapable connection between God's pity for our spiritual depravity and our pity for others' physical needs. The apostle John uses Jesus's sacrifice, which has predominantly spiritual significance, as the reason we should care for the physical needs for others with our material possessions. John does not pause to explain the connection between the two types of needs; he simply assumes it.

Looking back, before Jesus's death and into his three years of ministry, it is easy to see why John would assume that his audience will make the connection. Jesus's compassion led him to meet both physical and spiritual needs, seemingly without preference. Consider, for example, the two verses below. They describe nearly identical circumstances; however, notice how Jesus's compassion takes a different form in each.

When Jesus landed and saw a large crowd, he had compassion on them and healed their sick.

—MATTHEW 14:14

When Jesus landed and saw a large crowd, he had compassion on them, because they were like sheep without a shepherd. So he began teaching them many things.

—MARK 6:34

The twofold nature of compassion was likewise expressed in Jesus parables. For example, at the close of the parable of the prodigal son, we see the Father's compassion inspiring forgiveness and restoration

---

[216] Two Greek words are translated into the single English word compassion. The first Greek word, splagchnon, literally means the inward parts (e.g., heart, liver, lungs, etc.). Figuratively, it can be taken as the birthplace of emotions, like affection or tenderness. The second Greek word, oiktirmos, is derived from the root word, oiktos, meaning pity. Information taken from Thomas, *Dictionaries.*

analogous to God's saving grace on us, his rebellious creation.[217] We see the same connection between compassion and forgiveness in the parable of the unmerciful servant.[218] In contrast to both of these parables is that of the Good Samaritan, whose exemplary compassion finds its outlet in alleviating a man's physical suffering alone.[219]

There is no indication, in Jesus's words or his deeds, that he saw meeting either physical or spiritual needs as the *real* point of ministry. They were part of the same mission, with neither being a second-class citizen. Rather than setting a person's physical and spiritual maladies at odds with one another, he often cared for them simultaneously. As Matthew records:

> *Jesus went through all the towns and villages, teaching in their synagogues, preaching the good news of the kingdom, and healing every disease and sickness. When he saw the crowds, he had compassion on them, because they were harassed and helpless, like sheep without a shepherd.*

—MATTHEW 9:35–36

This may be getting redundant, but it is important to understand the connection because we, as individuals and a church, have strayed far from Jesus's example and the teachings in Scripture. Instead of preserving a Christlike balance between meeting physical and spiritual needs, we seem to be making every effort to drive a wedge between them by elevating one above the other. Let us examine how our imbalances come about.

Compassion for Physical Suffering

Physical suffering is both easier to see and easier to fix than spiritual suffering, so we will start here. It can be thought of in

---

[217] Luke 15:20–24.
[218] Matthew 18:21–35.
[219] Luke 10:30–35.

terms of both acute and chronic needs, with acute needs requiring brief interventions and chronic needs requiring long-term support. The types of physical needs we see Jesus meeting most often are of the acute variety—healing the sick and feeding hungry crowds. We tend to focus on these kinds of needs, too, whether because of Jesus's example or the fact that these brief interventions fit well into our busy schedules.

Of course, if we stick around acute needs long enough or go to places where they are more prevalent, we will begin to find the line between acute and chronic blurred. The vast majority of acute needs are not the result of famines, droughts, plagues, hurricanes, tsunamis, or any other one-time natural catastrophe. Rather, most find their roots in chronic and systemic issues like injustice, oppression, and poverty.

While Jesus did not devote much time to meeting chronic needs directly, it is clear from the rest of Scripture that God expects his people, whom he indwells, to be actively working out his mercy and justice on the earth in ways that address chronic issues. Israel is a prime example. Their apathy to the plight of the marginalized— orphans, widows, and aliens—ultimately led to their rejection and destruction by God.[220] While they faithfully practiced religion, with sacrifices and festivals and prayers, no amount of religious activity could cover over their failure to seek out and alleviate systemic physical suffering.

Praise the Lord that there are many in the church today who long for a deeper, more active faith and desire to give folks compassion they can feel, not just hear about. However, we must be careful here. Our zeal for justice and mercy has a way of outrunning Christ, into the arms of men like Gandhi and women like Mother Teresa who, though lacking overt concern for the state of the souls around them,[221] look to have, in abundance, the

---

[220] Isaiah 1:13,15–17.

[221] Neither Gandhi nor Mother Teresa, it seems, believed in Christ as *the* means of salvation and thus did not strive to bring others to a saving faith in him. For example, although a professing Christian, Mother Teresa wrote, "I've always said we should help a Hindu become a better Hindu, a Muslim become a better Muslim, a Catholic become a better Catholic" (Mother Teresa, *A Simple Path* [New York, NY: Random House, 1995], 31).

fruits of the Spirit that we find so lacking in our local body of believers.

The crucial mistake here is to view the alleviation of physical suffering as our *primary* means of expanding God's kingdom. When we create that kind of priority list in the face of boundless need, we end up pouring all of our limited time, energy, and resources into changing people's earthly situations with nothing left to care for their spiritual distress.

Of course, we have ways of covering our imbalance. Mantras like "Preach the gospel at all times; when necessary, use words,"[222] are well-worn enough to convince us that giving a cup of cold water to the thirsty man is a reasonable substitute for an offer of living water that might "become in him a spring of water welling up to eternal life."[223]

Truth can also become inconvenient when the primary goal is alleviating physical suffering. For while truly destitute folks—those dying of hunger, thirst, or nakedness—do not often turn away help, hopeless sinners will do just that to avoid the good news of eternal life in Jesus Christ. We can see this on the grand scale in third-world governmental policies that welcome medical aid, business investments, and educational initiatives, but only so far as they are divorced of any connection to the gospel. We can also see it in the lives of individuals who welcome our friendship as long as we are bringing them meals or repairing their home, but grow cold and silent when we invite them to submit themselves wholly to the loving rule of King Jesus.

Jesus knew that tolerance was much more convenient than truth, even when truth was offered out of loving compassion, but

---

[222] This phrase is commonly attributed to St. Francis of Assisi. However as Mark Galli, author of a biography on St. Francis, writes, "He did not say it. Nor did he live it." The saying did not appear until some two hundred years after St. Francis's death, and while he was alive, St. Francis faithfully preached the word of God (sometimes to as many as five different towns in one day). "He denounced evil whenever he found it," Galli quotes an early biographer as writing, "and made no effort to palliate it; from him a life of sin met with outspoken rebuke, not support." From *"Speak the Gospel: Use deeds when necessary"* by Mark Galli, *Christianity Today*, May 21, 2009, access date October 15, 2011, http://www.christianitytoday.com/ct/2009/mayweb-only/120-42.0.html.

[223] John 4:17.

that did not change his ministry.[224] While Jesus loved the world and healed countless folks, he was hated. He was not hated for joining with the poor around him or loving unconditionally (as some have suggested);[225] those kinds of things garnered him huge crowds. Instead, he was hated and ultimately killed because the claims he made about himself rocked the boat of culture and tradition. Jesus warned his followers to expect the same kind of treatment.

If the world hates you, keep in mind that it hated me first. If you belonged to the world, it would love you as its own. As it is, you do not belong to the world, but I have chosen you out of the world. That is why the world hates you.

—JOHN 15:18–19

The early believers were indeed hated by the world. While their generous compassion for physical needs both inside and out of the body of believers earned them "favor with all men," their unshakable and well-defined gospel message earned them beatings, imprisonments, and even death. They lost possessions, homes, and loved ones, all for the sake of advancing the kingdom of heaven in the hearts of the men and women around them.

Take Peter and John, for example. Shortly after Pentecost they were walking to the temple when they came across a beggar who had been crippled from birth. Peter's compassion led him to heal the man "in the name of Jesus Christ of Nazareth." When folks were amazed at the healing, Peter and John did not shy away from the attention out of false humility or fear, but instead, they seized the opportunity to put the spotlight on Jesus, whose kingdom rule the crowd had so recently and emphatically rejected.

---

[224] Tolerance no longer means living peaceably among people of conflicting ideas, but accepting the rather baffling proposition that we can all believe in contradictory ideas and yet all be right at the same time. We conveniently disregard the logical inconsistencies, not because anything about the world is fundamentally different, but because it takes away from the uncomfortable need to speak truth into the lives of others.

[225] Shane Claiborne, *The Irresistible Revolution* (Grand Rapids, MI: Zondervan, 2006), 144.

You disowned the Holy and Righteous One and asked that a murderer be released to you. You killed the author of life, but God raised him from the dead. We are witnesses of this....Repent, then, and turn to God, so that your sins may be wiped out, that times of refreshing may come from the Lord, and that he may send the Christ, who has been appointed for you—even Jesus....Anyone who does not listen to him will be completely cut off from among his people.

—Acts 3:14–15, 19–20, 23

The religious leaders of Jerusalem jailed Peter and John for this outburst. Later, they were hauled in front of the courts and asked, "By what power or what name did you do this?" While this was the same court that had orchestrated Jesus's crucifixion, Peter and John did not back down from the message. Instead, Peter gave the religious leaders all the truth they could handle.

Rulers and elders of the people! If we are being called to account today for an act of kindness shown to a cripple and are asked how he was healed, then know this, you and all the people of Israel: It is by the name of Jesus Christ of Nazareth, whom you crucified but whom God raised from the dead, that this man stands before you healed. He is "the stone you builders rejected, which has become the capstone." Salvation is found in no one else, for there is no other name under heaven given to men by which we must be saved.

—Acts 4:8–12

The exclusivity in that last line of Peter's speech is impossible to miss. If Peter's primary reference point or means of kingdom expansion had been to heal folks, then there would have been no cause to make a stand for the name of Jesus Christ. He would have welcomed the opportunity to heal but kept his mouth shut when the crowd got excited. After all, why risk death or rejection when silence would have guaranteed him another day to fight sickness and injustice on Jesus's behalf?

Peter proclaimed the truth about Christ because, when it comes to entrance into the kingdom of heaven, a certain amount of audible intolerance is required. Jesus alone can save us from our sins, bringing us out of de-creation into his glorious presence. Allah cannot do this, nor can a Christ-less Yaweh or Buddha or Krishna. At some point, we who pride ourselves on being the hands of Christ to a hurting world have to own the reality that people must be taught explicitly about Jesus to be saved by him.[226]

Compassion for Spiritual Suffering

Spiritual suffering can be harder to spot than physical depravity, whether because of well-constructed facades or the overwhelming drama of a life in physical shambles. Add that to the fact that we cannot cause spiritual change on our own, and we can see why it can be hard for some to get excited about sharing truth with others. Of course, if what Peter said is true—"There is no other name under heaven given to men by which we must be saved"—then silence may just be one of the most unloving and compassionless things we can offer another human being.

Imagine, by way of analogy, that there is a canyon near where you live. A bridge once spanned the canyon, but years ago it collapsed and was never rebuilt. A road still leads out to the bridge, and though at different times folks have tried to barricade it, the obstacles have always been removed as quickly as they were put up. Now suppose you are driving near that road when you see an out-of-towner take the turn toward the bridge. Would it be loving for you to leave them undisturbed and go on about your day as usual, or does compassion for their inevitable demise demand that you do everything you can to warn them about the faulty bridge and the deadly canyon?

---

[226] See also John 9:36; Acts 8:31; and Romans 10:14.

In a very imperfect way, this analogy describes our call, as re-created beings, to multiply God's rule in a de-created world. Remember, the only alternative to re-created life with Christ forever is de-created life apart from Christ forever, suffering in the lake of fire. Love does not win when we ignore the imminent reality of eternal suffering. Rather, love wins when we invite others off that broad road that leads to destruction and onto the straight and narrow path of submission to King Jesus. He himself said, "I am the way and the truth and the life. No one comes to the Father except through me."[227]

Still we can run into a problem if we let our zeal for truth outshine the other aspects of image bearing that we were created to hold in balance. Whether we make doctrine our priority because we find great delight in nailing down the finer points of theology or simply because we fear the influence of the so-called "social gospel," the result is the same. Our scarce resources are quickly exhausted in the face of the world's limitless spiritual depravity, with nothing left for other "lesser" ministries.

We may have nothing personal against compassion for physical needs and can even happily applaud those who do feel a particular call to share Christ in this way. But if, in our minds and lives, gospel truth is predominantly if not solely a matter of words, this becomes our unassailable excuse for the fact that compassion for physical needs finds no place in our creeds or our budgets.

In the end, however, the very words of Scripture that we readily defend and that we so wish to see transform others' hearts will stand in judgment of our lives. As we saw in 1 John 3:16–18, no response to Jesus's sacrifice is complete without laying down our material lives for the material needs of our brothers and sisters.[228] Jesus offers the same indictment of merciless living when he describes the final judgment of the unfaithful:

> *Then he will say to those on his left, "Depart from me, you who are cursed, into the eternal fire prepared for the devil and his angels.*

---

[227] John 14:6.
[228] 1 John 3:16–18.

For I was hungry and you gave me nothing to eat, I was thirsty and you gave me nothing to drink, I was a stranger and you did not invite me in, I needed clothes and you did not clothe me, I was sick and in prison and you did not look after me."

They also will answer, "Lord, when did we see you hungry or thirsty or a stranger or needing clothes or sick or in prison, and did not help you?"

He will reply, "I tell you the truth, whatever you did not do for one of the least of these, you did not do for me."

— MATTHEW 25:41–45

Compassion for physical needs does not earn us heaven but it is the inevitable result of the Spirit dwelling within us. Remember, God trees bear God fruit. If we are not actively engaged in meeting the physical needs around us, we prove that Jesus is not our true King. In that case, we will be rejected much like Israel was in the Old Testament and like the unrighteousness goats that Jesus describes above.

Our compassion for others' physical suffering accomplishes two important things toward alleviating their spiritual suffering as well. First, it provides the world with an accurate reflection of the King to whom we are calling them to give their lives. Second, our compassion removes physical barriers to the gospel message, such as homelessness, joblessness, slavery, illiteracy, and addiction. Yes, the Holy Spirit does work in spite of these barriers, but it is foolish to ignore the obvious strain these factors place on a person's ability to hear, receive, and grow in the gospel.

Until resourced believers have struggled alongside those believers who are among the impoverished, defenseless margin that bears the vast majority of society's ills, we will find it extremely hard to appreciate the cost of the instability that injustice spawns. Our unquestioning pursuit of the world's self-insulating reference points of comfort and security will ensure that poverty and other systemic injustices never get so close to us as to cross the threshold of our moral proximity,[229] thus remaining safely somebody else's problem and somebody else's fault. From that kind of distance, it can be easy to forget that a gospel void of intentional and tangible concern for the physical well-being of our brothers and sisters is worthless to us and to them.[230]

A Christlike Balance

We have already examined the example of our King, whose compassion led him to alleviate both the physical and spiritual distress around him, seemingly without preference. We have also examined the marching orders he has left for us in his Word, the Bible, which carry with them the same inseparable connection between the physical and the spiritual that Jesus modeled. Together, the commands and the model of Christ seem to be enough evidence to throw out any notion of priority within compassion and simultaneously set about alleviating the physical *and* spiritual suffering of our believing and unbelieving neighbors.

For those of us primarily concerned with physical suffering, we must cultivate a sense of urgency in reaching the spiritually lost around us. We must remind ourselves of both the glorious love and the terrible judgment of our King, again and again, until we have built up enough conviction to proclaim truth at every opportunity without regard for the cost. As we are faithfully bearing witness to Jesus, we must also learn to trust him with the results, recognizing that only he can bring his kingdom about in our hearts and in the hearts of those around us.

If we find ourselves in this camp, it may be helpful to consider a few questions as individuals:

---

[229] "Moral proximity refers to how connected we are to someone by virtue of familiarity, kinship, space, or time....The closer the moral proximity, the greater the moral obligation" (Kevin DeYoung and Greg Gilbert, *What Is the Mission of the Church?* [Wheaton, IL: Crossway, 2011], 183).

[230] James 2:16–18.

- Could I explain the basic components of the gospel to someone? When is the last time I did?
- Am I seeking to get into conversations about God, or do I only talk about him when others initiate?
- Am I willing to endure awkward moments and ruined friendships to give people a chance at life?

Those of us who pride ourselves on being champions for truth and doctrine must learn to also live out God's compassion for the physical depravity of the marginalized and oppressed. This will be hard, particularly if we are upwardly mobile, with resources and opportunities. Friends and family will urge us to avoid those places where physical afflictions are most prevalent. Such places are less safe, with fewer jobs, more substandard schools, and depressed housing markets. Who in their right mind seeks out those things for themselves or their families?

True believers are happy to admit that they do not have a right *earthly* state of mind. They are focused on Christ above, and expanding his heavenly rule on earth is their default mode of operation. When it comes time to choose locations, relationships, jobs, hobbies, and so forth, believers do so according to what best positions them to bear the whole image of God and teach others to do the same. If we find ourselves focusing on spiritual needs, we should consider how we might get back to Christlike balance by asking ourselves a few questions:

- Where are the marginalized—orphans, fatherless, foreigners, widows, homeless, addicts, mentally ill, or disabled—around me? How can I adopt, stand up for, or otherwise support one or more of them? What would keep me from doing so?
- Have I hidden my addictions to money, comfort, success, and safety behind an outspoken concern for the spiritual depravity around me? If so, what pos-

sessions can I give away or sell so that I may help
meet the needs of others?

Compassion is part of our new wardrobe as image bearers, and
we cannot take our place in the kingdom of heaven without it. Nor
can we willingly accept a partial expression of it in our lives. As
God's chosen people, holy and dearly loved, we must put on his
compassion for the spiritually and physically poor of our world.[231]
We do so simultaneously, without forcing apart and separately prioritizing what God has so clearly left connected in his Word and in
the life of his son, Jesus Christ. This is for God's glory and our joy.

---

[231] Isaiah 58:10.

12

Humility and Gentleness

Therefore, as God's chosen people, holy and dearly loved, clothe yourselves with...humility, gentleness...

—Colossians 3:12

The image of Christ ruling on the throne of heaven is entirely about him. Christ is the all-powerful, all-good, self-existent, and self-sufficient Creator and King. That is the image we are to fix our hearts and minds on, and it should inspire deep humility in our rebellious hearts. See, for example, how the throne room experience affected the prophet Isaiah.

In the year that King Uzziah died, I saw the Lord seated on a throne, high and exalted, and the train of his robe filled the temple. Above him were seraphs, each with six wings: With two wings they covered their faces, with two they covered their feet, and with two they were flying. And they were calling to one another:

"Holy, holy, holy is the Lord Almighty;
the whole earth is full of his glory."

At the sound of their voices the doorposts and thresholds shook, and
the temple was filled with smoke.

"Woe to me!" I cried. "I am ruined! For I am a man of unclean
lips, and I live among a people of unclean lips, and my eyes have
seen the King, the Lord Almighty."

—ISAIAH 6:1–5

Humility is the proper appreciation for our smallness next to God's greatness, and our sinfulness next to his holiness. It is a prerequisite for loving God and others appropriately, for only when we recognize our own depravity will we be able to answer the command to hold the interests of other broken sinners above our own.[232]

Though humility takes cultivation, it has always been a defining mark of God's true subjects. One such example is John the Baptist. His life and teachings provide some wonderful insight into the practical connection between humility and the Christ-first focus of the true believer.

They came to John and said to him, "Rabbi, that man who was
with you on the other side of the Jordan—the one you testified
about—well, he is baptizing, and everyone is going to him."

To this John replied, "A man can receive only what is given him
from heaven. You yourselves can testify that I said, 'I am not
the Christ but am sent ahead of him.' The bride belongs to the
bridegroom. The friend who attends the bridegroom waits and
listens for him, and is full of joy when he hears the bridegroom's

---

[232] In many ways, humility, which leads to gentleness, is the equal and opposite virtue to the self-focused love that leads to the "anger, rage, malice, slander, and filthy language" spoken of in Colossians 3:8. See also Philippians 2:3–4.

voice. That joy is mine, and it is now complete. He must become greater; I must become less."

—*JOHN 3:26–30*

John's preeminent reference point in life was Jesus Christ. He did what he did and said what he said primarily because of its beneficial effect on the advancement of Jesus's kingdom. John the Baptist found his worth in Jesus, and out of this humble perspective flowed joyful and powerful witness. Without regard for his own well-being or comfort, he preached about the sin around him and the need for repentance. He did not make much of himself, but pointed all of his followers back to Jesus.[233]

Notice the practical effect of John's single-minded gaze on Jesus. When John's ministry was losing members, what was his reaction? Did he weep and moan? No. He rejoiced! Did he worry about losing financial or material support? No. He rejoiced! Did he start a turf war with the ministries around him? No. He rejoiced! Did he change his message? No. He rejoiced! For John, success had nothing to do with numbers and everything to do with faithful witness. His joy was entirely wrapped up in serving his King.

What would a church with the humility of John the Baptist look like? A people who thought so little of themselves in the face of the opportunity to share the truths of the kingdom of God would certainly look strange, even without the camel hair. While there are undoubtedly folks who do this well, it is easy wander from John's example, either because we are so distracted by our increasing knowledge of Christ that we fall into self-righteousness or because we are driven by our timidity into an ungodly state of hidden humility.

Distracted by Self-Righteousness

Let us deal with the false reference point of knowledge first. To be clear, there is nothing wrong with knowledge of Jesus. It is the

---

[233] John 1:29.

means by which we are transformed into the likeness of our Creator, and thus sound doctrine should be encouraged and developed in the body of Christ. What we must be careful to avoid doing is making a false reference point of knowledge by adding our preferences onto the gospel or by limiting our faith to the endless consumption and regurgitation of facts.

Not adding ourselves onto the gospel can be hard. As we mature in Christ, we invariably adopt specific behaviors that help us to maintain holiness. That in itself is profitable for the kingdom, and it would be great if we could just stop there. Over time, however, we can start to think that these behaviors have worth in themselves; we can believe that we somehow can do or say things that earn us favor with God. From there, it does not take long before we begin extending our convictions and methods onto others.

The gospel is a good start, we think, but it would be better if only others shared our particular, extra-biblical conviction about speaking in tongues or becoming cross-cultural missionaries or reading theology or moving to a poor inner city. At that point, the gospel ceases to be about Jesus and becomes about our form of self-righteousness. We prop ourselves up on pedestals built out of piety or social concern or theological mastery or deconstructed worship. People can see us better, but not God.

I attended a Christian conference a number of years ago where this issue of self-righteousness obscuring God's truth came into play. The conference was put on by a father-son duo whose ability to explain and defend the truths of election and the sovereignty of God is equaled by few. Initially, I was very excited to hear them speak. However, rather than teaching during the first session, they spent much of the time ridiculing those who did not agree with them and laughingly dismissing the thoughts of other well-meaning Christians. After that, my excitement was gone.

The ability to teach about God's sovereignty had become a thing these men lorded over those around them. The theological arguments were sound, but their hearts were far from humble, and instead, reminiscent of the Pharisees of Jesus's day. While they spoke of the glories of Jesus Christ, they made seemingly no effort to let that glory permeate their lives. The Christ who must be all was relegated to a sliver of head knowledge, and without loving humility, even that came across as empty chatter.

Sadly, the crowd laughed right along. Even more saddening is the reality that these two men are not alone and this crowd is not unique. We often not only tolerate but even celebrate such haughtiness in the church, particularly if the person is skilled at what they do. We also delight in sarcasm itself, especially when it comes at the expense of our enemies (inside the body of Christ or not). But why? Why do we tolerate haughtiness rather than putting it to death as we are commanded?

If we are to move forward, we must begin to understand gentleness, which is born out of humility.[234] Gentleness seems to be the Scriptural antithesis to the harsh and haughty rebukes of the self-righteous, as virtually every use of it in the New Testament deals with the idea of correcting or training someone in righteousness.[235] Take, for example, Paul's words to Timothy:

> *Those who oppose {the Lord's servant} he must gently instruct, in the hope that God will grant them repentance leading them to a knowledge of the truth.*
>
> —2 TIMOTHY 2:25

For those of us who pride ourselves on "saying it like it is," gentleness will not come easily. While we prefer to be blunt, we must also be discerning. This does not mean we go to the other extreme of timidity, but we would be wise to ask ourselves a few questions before we speak.

---

[234] Though most often translated as "gentleness," the same word, prautēs, is translated elsewhere as "humility" (James 1:21) and "meekness" (2 Corinthians 10:1).

[235] 1 Corinthians 4:21; 2 Corinthians 10:1; Galatians 6:1; 2 Timothy 2:25; 1 Peter 3:15.

- Am I sharing truth in a way that is honest yet consistent with other Christlike virtues of kindness and peace?
- Am I sharing truth to build up my hearers in Christ or tear them down?
- Have I prayed for the Holy Spirit to guide me and speak through me? Have I sought out the sharpening of the Lord's Word and his people?

In our truth telling, we ought to emulate Jesus, who is both the bold Lion of Judah and the gentle Lamb of God. This is not a balance we can conjure up on our own. It can only come from the Holy Spirit himself, who, being of the same nature as Jesus, is both the "spirit of power" and the spirit "of love."[236] Because the Spirit lives in every believer and eagerly desires to bear his fruit in each of us, we have but to yield to him to see Christlike truth spoken through us in Christlike gentleness.[237]

Distracted by Timidity

Some of us are not bold or self-confident. We love the praise of others and at the same time fear their reproach. While we may recognize our timidity as a problem, we can just as easily begin to excuse it in the name of humility. One look at John the Baptist, however, and our guise is undone. His fittingly low view of himself in relation to Christ was coupled with a very visible and outspoken ministry on Christ's behalf. Jesus further undoes our excuses, as we saw in chapter nine, teaching that visibility is essential for true disciples:

You are the light of the world. A city on a hill cannot be hidden. Neither do people light a lamp and put it under a bowl. Instead they put it on its stand, and it gives light to everyone in the house.

---

[236] 2 Timothy 1:7.

[237] Romans 8:9; Galatians 5:16–26.

In the same way, let your light shine before men, that they may see your good deeds and praise your Father in heaven.

—MATTHEW 5:14–16

Disciples do not merely reflect light; we become it, in Christ. Through the power of Holy Spirit, we become the righteousness of God and agents of reconciliation who act to preserve those around us for eternity by illuminating truth.[238] As author and professor Dr. Robert Coleman writes:

> *Jesus went on to show his disciples "that repentance and remission of sin should be preached in his name unto all nations, beginning from Jerusalem" (Luke 24:47). And for the fulfillment of this divine purpose, the disciples were no less a part than their Master. They were to be the human instruments announcing the good tidings, and the Holy Spirit was to be God's personal empowerment for their mission. "Ye shall receive power when the Holy Ghost is come upon you: and ye shall be my witnesses both in Jerusalem, and in all Judea and Samaria, and unto the uttermost part of the earth" (Acts 1:8; cf., Luke 24:48, 49).*[239]

The danger in hiding our light—in failing to bear God's image and make disciples—is that the world never gets to know about its Creator through the witness and example of his body. Jesus can work salvation through miraculous methods. That much is undeniable. Story after story can be told of unreached peoples coming to Christ by direct messages or visions from the King himself. However, Dr. Coleman reminds us, these stories are exceptions to the equally undeniable rule of kingdom expansion through discipleship.

---

[238] 2 Corinthians 5:17–21.

[239] *The Master Plan of Evangelism* (Peabody, MA: Prince Press, 2000), 87.

It all came back to his disciples. They were the vanguard of his enveloping movement. "Through their word" he expected others to believe in him (John 17:20), and these in turn to pass the word along to others, until in time the world might know who he was and what he came to do (John 17:21, 23). His whole evangelistic strategy—indeed, the fulfillment of his very purpose in coming into the world, dying on the cross, and rising from the grave—depended on the faithful witness of his chosen disciples to this task. It did not matter how small the group was to start with so long as they reproduced and taught their disciples to reproduce. This was the way the church was to win—through the dedicated lives of those who knew the Savior so well that his Spirit and method constrained them to tell others. As simple as it may seem, this was the way the gospel would conquer. He had no other plan.[240]

Certainly, the call to humility creates a certain tension with the call to visible righteousness, but that does not mean we do away with either one. Instead, every Christian must fight to maintain this tension because through it we remain humble in the face of increasing holiness. While letting our deeds shine before men, we do not let them shine before ourselves. Instead they rise as an offering to our King. This is the blindness to self that keeps our right hand from knowing what our left is doing.[241] When our gaze is resting on Christ, we have no time to waste looking at ourselves. Bonhoeffer described faithful humility in the following terms:

From whom are we to hide the visibility of our discipleship? Certainly not from other men, for we are told to let them see our light. No. We are to hide it from ourselves. Our task is simply to keep on following, looking only to our Leader who goes on before, taking no notice of ourselves or of what we are doing. We must

[240] Coleman, *Evangelism*, 99.

[241] Matthew 6:3.

be unaware of our own righteousness, and see it only in so far as we look unto Jesus; then it will seem not extraordinary, but quite ordinary and natural.[242]

How will we put ordinary kingdom humility into practice? Consider the following questions to get you started:

- Have I accepted my state as a fallen creature, utterly dependent on the mercy of my Creator, or do I entertain thoughts of earning God's favor through Christian activities or serving others?
- Am I able, like John the Baptist, to rejoice when faithful Christians leave my ministry to go to another where they will be more useful?
- Do I submit to correction from friends and authority figures? Do I seek out correction even when others are not offering it openly?
- Do I look down on other Christians who do not agree with me? How might I encourage them, even if I continue to disagree with them?

At the end of the day, our inspiration for humility is Christ himself. As Paul wrote to the Philippians:

Your attitude should be the same as that of Christ Jesus: Who, being in very nature God, did not consider equality with God something to be grasped, but made himself nothing, taking the very nature of a servant, being made in human likeness. And being found in appearance as a man, he humbled himself and became obedient to death—even death on a cross!

—PHILIPPIANS 2:5–8

---

[242] *Discipleship*, 158.

We ought to remind ourselves of that example as often as we can—the example of our glorious and all-powerful and all-loving God, who not only created us but redeemed us from our sinful misery and continues to faithfully sanctify us. Then, when our dreams of the good life or expectations of immediate convenience stand in the way of being most effective for God's kingdom, through his grace we will be able to say with our Lord Jesus, "Yet not as I will, but as you will."[243] Such is the relationship of a slave to the King. We who were bought at a price ought never to think otherwise.

---

[243] Matthew 26:39.

13

Patience

Therefore, as God's chosen people, holy and dearly loved, clothe yourselves with...patience.

—COLOSSIANS 3:12

L ove for God and others requires unusually great patience on behalf of God's people. While the world settles for a patience that bears "pains or trials calmly or without complaint" and stands firm "despite opposition, difficulty, or adversity,"[244] Jesus demands more of his disciples. Christlike patience does not passively accept trials as inevitabilities of a broken life but transforms them into opportunities for refinement and rejoicing.[245]

Trouble, of course, is not unique to Christians. Since the fall, creation has been subjected to every form of frustration. It has turned on itself and on us, for whom God lovingly prepared it. Every year brings more earthquakes, tsunamis, hurricanes, floods, tornadoes, droughts, famines, and disease. If that were not enough,

---

[244] Merriam-Webster.
[245] Matthew 13:44–46; 2 Corinthians 4:17; 1 Peter 1:7; 5:1.

we humans have turned on one another as well. We murder, rape, and oppress others. We steal and destroy what is not ours. In "civilized" societies, we move from the physical attacks to verbal ones and from open oppression to systemic injustice.

Yet even while humanity feels suffering universally, it is also true that Christians are promised an additional measure of persecution for the sake of the gospel that we preach.[246] As we have already seen Jesus explain to his disciples:

> If the world hates you, keep in mind that it hated me first. If you belonged to the world, it would love you as its own. As it is, you do not belong to the world, but I have chosen you out of the world. That is why the world hates you. Remember the words I spoke to you: "No servant is greater than his master." If they persecuted me, they will persecute you also. If they obeyed my teaching, they will obey yours also.

—JOHN 15:18–20

Jesus's disciples did indeed go on to experience much persecution. Scripture records that early Christians were publicly exposed to insult and persecution, their property was seized, and they were beaten or imprisoned. Many died horribly painful deaths rather than forsake the gospel.[247] The apostle Paul was no stranger to suffering for the gospel, as he explained to the believers in Corinth:

> Five times I received from the Jews the forty lashes minus one. Three times I was beaten with rods, once I was stoned, three times I was shipwrecked, I spent a night and a day in the open sea, I have been constantly on the move. I have been in danger from rivers, in danger from bandits, in danger from my own countrymen, in danger from Gentiles; in danger in the city, in danger in the country, in danger at sea; and in danger from false brothers. I have labored and toiled

---

[246] 2 Timothy 3:12.

[247] For examples see chapter one of *Foxe's Book of Martyrs* by John Foxe.

*and have often gone without sleep; I have known hunger and thirst
and have often gone without food; I have been cold and naked.
Besides everything else, I face daily the pressure of my concern for
all the churches. Who is weak, and I do not feel weak?*

—2 Corinthians 11:24–29

Paul's resume is impressive. Very few Christians have, or ever
will, match Paul's trials either in quality or quantity. Even more
impressive than the kind of sufferings Paul endured is the attitude
with which he endured them. Take, for example, when he and Silas
were attacked by a crowd, stripped naked, and "severely flogged"
before being thrown into jail with their feet placed in stocks.
Amazingly, while blood still seeped from open wounds on their
backs, they began to sing praises to God and did so loud enough for
the other prisoners to hear.[248]

By earthly standards, Paul and Silas were clearly insane. No sen-
sible worldling would ever act as they did in those circumstances.
Yet it seems that their "insanity" was nothing more than the common, heavenly minded patience that allows God's people to fulfill
their call to consider trials as pure joy. See how Jesus describes his
expectations:

*Blessed {literally "happy"} are you when people insult you, persecute
you and falsely say all kinds of evil against you because of me.
Rejoice and be glad, because great is your reward in heaven, for in
the same way they persecuted the prophets who were before you.*

—Matthew 5:11–12

In the kingdom of heaven, virtually everything gets turned around
and flipped upside-down, including the way we value people and
circumstances. For the believer, chosen by God to be holy and dearly
loved, there ceases to be a *bad* circumstance because "in all things

---

[248] Acts 16:16–40.

God works for the good of those who love him, who have been called according to his purpose."[249] Not only does God promise to carry us, his children, through evil and suffering and death, he has ordained *each* instance of these to be for his glory and our joy.[250]

Distracted by Stoicism

No matter how many times we read the command to "rejoice and be glad," it can still be tempting to think that Jesus surely meant for us to "grin and bear it." Otherwise Jesus's expectations are impossible, right? He was just setting an idealized goal, one that he never expected us to follow, right? Forget Paul and Silas, we say. All Jesus really demands of us is that we adopt an attitude of noble and stoic indifference to pain. We think that we beat suffering by outlasting it and cement such beliefs with constant repetition of pithy, though unbiblical, sayings such as "This too shall pass."

While such gritty, stone-faced determination may earn the respect of our neighbors, it comes nowhere near the kind of hope-filled patience that flows from a Christian's focus on the King who is both able to provide for his people and eagerly does so in every circumstance. Instead of pointing folks to our very great reward, we settle for earthly versions of patience, which only ever reinforce earthly ideals such as self-sufficiency and self-discipline.

Consider how we react to trials. Is our aim to get through trials or to joyfully embrace them as opportunities to advance the kingdom? What happens when a spouse leaves, a job is lost, we grow ill, or a loved one dies? How do we react when we fail a test or crash a car or when we are laughed at for our faith or our looks? Do we rejoice and thank God, or do we try to figure a way out on our own, all the while cursing our bad luck? What about situations that simply make us mad; what would it take to thank God for those?

Now think about those around us. What hope do we offer them? What do we say to the mother who has lost a child? How can

---

[249] Romans 8:28.

[250] Isaiah 45:7.

we console the dad who cannot find a job to support his family even after months of searching? What words do we offer children who have experienced physical, emotional, or sexual abuse or the friend whose parent has been diagnosed with terminal cancer? What about the couple who, in order to proclaim the gospel, moved to a place where it is neither heard nor felt, only to be held up at gunpoint in front of their home or have their possessions stolen?

Most of us probably shrink back from suffering, whether it is ours or someone else's. We are out of practice, so to speak, because our affluence allows us to limit our own suffering and to distance ourselves from suffering in others.[251] When trials do come, they seem random and inconvenient to our lives. Our first reaction is not usually joy but indignation. While God demands us to receive trials as discipline for our sanctification, we are like spoiled children fighting his discipline at every turn.[252]

At best, we manage to bear our own suffering silently. When it comes to others' suffering, however, our "grin and bear it" philosophy offers no hope. So we, like the pagans around us, fidget uncomfortably whenever the de-created state of our world is laid bare by pain and hardships. If there is a physical need to meet, then we happily do so, otherwise we are left believing that all we have to offer others is our sympathetic prayers for alleviation of their burden.

Distracted by Omens

Another way we can be distracted by life's trials is to view them as specific corrective actions. That is, when something bad happens, we interpret that circumstance as an omen of God's disfavor with any recent decisions or behaviors. One modern-day example of this would be to attribute the emergence of the disease HIV/AIDS entirely to the perceived coincident increase in promiscuity, fornication, and

---

[251] Believers should not seek suffering for suffering's sake. However, persecution is guaranteed for every true believer (Mark 10:30). It seems the more we focus our desires on Christ and the more Christlike we become, the more we will be persecuted (1 Peter 4:4; John 15:18–25).

[252] Hebrews 12:7.

homosexuality.[253] We are not alone in this error. Jesus's first disciples made it, too, and we can see how quickly and firmly he rebukes them:

> *Now there were some present at that time who told Jesus about the Galileans whose blood Pilate had mixed with their sacrifices. Jesus answered, "Do you think that these Galileans were worse sinners than all the other Galileans because they suffered this way? I tell you, no! But unless you repent, you too will all perish. Or those eighteen who died when the tower in Siloam fell on them—do you think they were more guilty than all the others living in Jerusalem? I tell you, no! But unless you repent, you too will all perish."*

> —LUKE 13:1–5

Jesus's point is that discipline through hardships is not necessarily aimed at punishing a specific behavior or decision. Rather, the purpose behind pain and suffering is to generally remind us of our finite nature and unequivocal need for God. That is why Jesus turns the attention from the suffering of others back onto the hearts of his audience not once, but twice, saying, "Unless you repent, you too will all perish."

We can also make the opposite error of thinking the pleasantness of our circumstances is a sign of God's favor with our lives. If our girlfriend thinks the world of us, then we assume that means we should be with her. If we get along with our neighbors, then we talk about having been given affirmation and peace by God regarding our decision about where we chose to live. The same can be said of getting regular promotions at work. If we enjoy success, then we speak of God as "opening doors," and if we run up against problems, then God is said to be "closing doors."

The obvious problem is that there have always been and will always be some hardened sinners who lead comfortable and

---

[253] The issue here is not so much that we recognize a connection between spreading sexually transmitted diseases and having multiple sexual partners. It is that we see the disease as a specific judgment from God, which implies that those of us who do not have the disease are still in God's favor.

phenomenally successful lives in worldly terms. Meanwhile, the lives of other unrepentant sinners consist of seemingly endless suffering. The same split is true of the righteous. Even when righteous people succeed in this world, Scripture is clear that this is not evidence that they are doing things according to God's will of desire.[254] As such, we would do well to heed the words of Solomon, who wrote:

> *When times are good, be happy; but when times are bad, consider: God has made the one as well as the other. Therefore, a man cannot discover anything about his future.*

> — *ECCLESIASTES 7:14*

Distracted by Vengeance

While it may be hard enough to view seemingly random trials as blessings, much of our pain in life will come from the intentional and spiteful behavior of others, and we should be prepared for that, too. In such situations, Jesus demands that we, out of our belief in an all-powerful, all-loving God who works everything out for our good, not only rejoice in persecutions, but that we also seek to heap blessings on our persecutors.[255] Consider his words:

> *You have heard that it was said, "Eye for eye, and tooth for tooth." But I tell you, Do not resist an evil person. If someone strikes you on the right cheek, turn to him the other also. And if someone wants to sue you and take your tunic, let him have your cloak as well. If someone forces you to go one mile, go with him two miles. Give*

---

[254] Consider the examples of Abraham and Isaac, who both lied about their wives being their sisters, and meanwhile were *rewarded* with great prosperity and lavish gifts of money and servants. At least once, the *blessings* were even the direct result of the lie. See Genesis 12:10–20; 20:1–18; 26:1–14.

[255] Proverbs 25:21–22; Romans 12:14, 17–21.

to the one who asks you, and do not turn away from the one who wants to borrow from you.

You have heard that it was said, "Love your neighbor and hate your enemy." But I tell you: Love your enemies and pray for those who persecute you, that you may be sons of your Father in heaven. He causes his sun to rise on the evil and the good, and sends rain on the righteous and the unrighteous. If you love those who love you, what reward will you get? Are not even the tax collectors doing that? And if you greet only your brothers, what are you doing more than others? Do not even pagans do that? Be perfect, therefore, as your heavenly Father is perfect.

—MATTHEW 5:38–48

We touched on the corresponding passage in Luke, briefly at the end of chapter ten, in our discussion of Christlike love for others. It serves as evidence that otherworldly love for others requires strangely gracious and active patience. While the world teaches us to fight back—either by force or law—when someone wrongs us, Jesus teaches us to be all the more generous and openhanded with that person. This is not a new command or even a replacement for an old one.[256]

Our enemies may present any number of ways. They may be physically violent toward us (verse 39) or seek our material harm through the auspices of the law (verse 40). They may take advantage of us through societal obligations (verse 41) or by not making good on their obligations to us (verse 42). They may simply be indifferent to us or God (verse 45), refusing to love us (verse 46) or even to greet us (verse 47). Whatever the case, our response is always to be godly patience, enduring their evil, while seeking their good.

While we may not find ourselves up against all the enemies that Jesus describes, we should take advantage of each opportunity

---

[256] Matthew 5:17. See also Romans 12:17–21 where Paul seamlessly connects Jesus's teachings with those written hundreds and hundreds of years earlier.

to do good as it arises. We must resist the urge to harm our enemies and instead choose to go beyond what is expected of us, even if they would never return the favor. Cold indifference is not to be ignored but greeted with winsome yet clear articulations of the gospel message along with warm invitations to experience Christ in the life of his people. We are to pray for the salvation of our enemies, that they might become friends for eternity.

A Kingdom-Inspired Patience

Examples of this kingdom-inspired patience are hard to find, but a woman in my church comes to mind. Karla is a young, single, black mother who was recently looking for a job. She had worked hard on her resume and had applied to a number of different positions. For a while nothing happened. After much prayer within the body, however, she landed a job in home healthcare and elder assistance.

When the day came for Karla to start, her new boss took her to the older women she was to begin caring for. It just so happened that this woman was white and had had some bad experiences in the past with black women. When Karla was introduced, the woman immediately began attacking her verbally. Karla wept as the woman assaulted her character based solely on her skin color, but did not say anything. Her new boss apologized profusely and offered to give Karla the next position that came along.

Many of us probably would have taken that offer, but Karla did not. The following week during our Sunday morning service, she asked for prayer that God would give her the strength and grace to work for this woman and to share his love with her. Can you imagine that? Karla not only forgave the woman who expressed so much hatred for her but also returned to the woman's home to wait on her and care for her.

As believers we ought all to likewise persevere in patience out of the hope that both we,[257] and our enemies[258] might be brought closer to Christ. Trials have a way of refining us in "the furnace of affliction."[259] Through God's grace, our impure distractions are burned away, and our vision of the King is perfected. In our unwavering hope, the world gets to re-experience its Lord, who "for the joy set before him endured the cross, scorning its shame, and sat down at the right hand of the throne of God."[260]

Let our patience be like the disciplined endurance of a marathon runner, who does not run aimlessly but stays the course and hits his prescribed pace, mile after mile.[261] While in one sense we endure for the joy set before us, remember, in Christ, we have already won and can even now run as a champion, rejoicing at the chance to run our course. Such patience must become as natural to the discipleship community as it is unnatural to the world around us.

We ought not excuse our frustrations with others and God or hide behind the pretense of righteous anger. We do not complain or argue.[262] Nor do we pity ourselves or fret when evil men succeed for a time.[263] Rather, we rejoice and are glad in every circumstance, for great is our reward in heaven. While our family, coworkers, friends, neighbors, and classmates chase after temporary pleasures and instant gratification, we wait for the Lord to fully re-create us and the world. Our hope is made sure as we persevere in the Word and carry on diligently to the very end.[264]

---

[257] Luke 21:19; Romans 2:7; Romans 8:25; 1 Thessalonians 1:3; James 1:12.

[258] Luke 8:15.

[259] Isaiah 48:10.

[260] Hebrews 12:2.

[261] Hebrews 12:1.

[262] Philippians 2:4.

[263] Psalm 37:7.

[264] Luke 8:15; Hebrews 6:12.

14

Bearing with and Forgiving

Bear with each other and forgive whatever grievances you may have against one another. Forgive as the Lord forgave you.

—COLOSSIANS 3:13

A s God's children, wholly and dearly loved, we have been declared righteous and holy in Christ. Our debt of sin has been paid completely, forever. But on earth, we still sin and will continue to do so until Christ returns at the end of time to make us fully new. This is not to say that we should do away with the sense of urgency with which we approach holiness, but to say that life is a progressive revelation of sin (to be put to death) and of the virtues of Christ (to be put on).

The implication of our progressive state of re-creation on earth is that the body of Christ is made up of individuals who are at various stages in the process of sanctification. As a result, we will inevitably hurt and be hurt by one another. To exist, let alone grow, as a body year after year requires the same patience and continual forgiveness we show unbelievers. Among believers, however, there is an additional component of bearing one another's burdens—in open confession, humble rebuke, willing repentance, and physical reprieve.

Neither forgiving others nor bearing their burdens comes naturally to us as fallen humans. For we are too easily distracted by our own pain and agendas to pick up our fellow believers, wounded and weighed down by sin as they are, and throw them over our shoulders until such a time as they can stand again to fight. We will explore the kingdom rationale for forgiveness and burden bearing shortly; however, let us first examine a few of the distractions that keep us from dealing with sin properly.

Distracted by Tolerance

In the kingdom of heaven, love simply cannot let people continue ignorantly down the path toward hell. As long as they will listen, the body of Christ humbly calls to its fellow sinners, warning them of the dangers of hell and encouraging them to grab hold of the glorious joy of life with the King. With professing believers, in particular, we have an obligation to maintain the holiness of the body by gently restoring those who have wandered from God's clearly defined will of desire. As Paul wrote to the Galatians:

> Brothers, if someone is caught in a sin, you who are spiritual should restore him gently. But watch yourself, or you also may be tempted. Carry each other's burdens, and in this way you will fulfill the law of Christ.

> —GALATIANS 6:1–2

Have you ever tried to do this? What happened? People probably got mad, right? People do not generally want to be called out on their sin. Instead of humbly submitting to correction, folks demand tolerance for sin and, perhaps, even start quoting Jesus when he said, "Let him who is without sin cast the first stone."[265] Maybe they even use Jesus's words from the beginning of Matthew 7:

Do not judge, or you too will be judged. For in the same way you judge others, you will be judged, and with the measure you use, it will be measured to you.

Why do you look at the speck of sawdust in your brother's eye and pay no attention to the plank in your own eye? How can you say to your brother, "Let me take the speck out of your eye," when all the time there is a plank in your own eye? You hypocrite, first take the plank out of your own eye, and then you will see clearly to remove the speck from your brother's eye.

—MATTHEW 7:1–5

Even folks who have never read a Bible seem to know these two passages by heart and cling to them as a sort of ace up the sleeve for that moment when someone gets a little too holy for their comfort. Everyone should keep their opinions and beliefs about sin and righteousness to themselves, right? Because we have made out faith to be personal and subjective, there is no transferable and objective standard by which to judge others. Even if there were, though, how could we as sinners ever be qualified to point out sin in others and exhort them toward righteousness?

At first glance this makes much sense, and better yet, it affirms our false worldly reference points of tolerance and convenience. The problem with this view, however, is that when we look at Scripture, it quickly becomes clear that there are also other passages (e.g., Galatians 6:1–2, seen above) which explicitly command Christians to address sin and judge others. Unless we are willing to say that the Bible contradicts itself, then we must then ask ourselves two questions: When is it wrong to judge and when is it right to judge?

If we go back to the passage from Matthew 7, Jesus clearly tells us not to judge because our own sinfulness (the "plank") has

---

[265] John 8:7.

blinded us. But the story does not stop there. Jesus wants us to get rid of the plank in our eye. Why? Well, he wants us to be able to remove the speck in our brother's eye. Thus, it seems Jesus's point is that judgment is wrong in the situation where we have sin that we have not confessed or repented of. Conversely, when we have openly put our own sin to death, we become fit for rebuking and encouraging our brothers and sisters for their good and for the good of the kingdom.

If Jesus does expect us to go back after we have dealt with our own sin, to help our fellow believers with their sin, then what standard should we use? Well, Jesus also says, "With the measure you use, it will be measured to you." Since we ourselves are judged by God's standards and these standards are revealed in the Bible for all to see, it makes sense that Christians should hold each other to this standard and not another one that we have made up. This is, again, why we must be absolutely certain that a person is violating God's standards (rather than our preferences or practical wisdom) when we rebuke them.[266]

God's desire from the very formation of his people was that they would live lives set apart from the world around them. He wanted his people to bear his image properly to the world, which is why so much of the Old Testament is devoted to defining righteousness and to recognizing and dealing with any sinful deviations from that standard. Though we are not under the Old Testament law, we have the same responsibility to live by God's standards, which is why Jesus talked so much about the need for sin and repentance. This brings us to another passage in Matthew.

If your brother sins against you, go and show him his fault, just between the two of you. If he listens to you, you have won your brother over. But if he will not listen, take one or two others along, so that "every matter may be established by the testimony of two or three witnesses." If he refuses to listen to them, tell it to the church;

---

[266] See also Romans 2:1–11.

*and if he refuses to listen even to the church, treat him as you would
a pagan or a tax collector.*

—MATTHEW 18:15–17

The command here, regarding a fellow believer in sin, is to "go
and show him his fault." Jesus is now explicitly instructing us to
judge others, not just allowing for it. We can see this intentional
intolerance of sin at work in the life of the early church, as Paul
rebukes the Corinthians:

*I have written you in my letter not to associate with sexually
immoral people—not at all meaning the people of this world who
are immoral, or the greedy and swindlers, or idolaters. In that
case you would have to leave this world. But now I am writing
you that you must not associate with anyone who calls himself
a brother but is sexually immoral or greedy, an idolater or a
slanderer, a drunkard or a swindler. With such a man do not
even eat.*

*What business is it of mine to judge those outside the church? Are
you not to judge those inside? God will judge those outside. "Expel
the wicked man from among you."*[267]

—1 CORINTHIANS 5:9–13

Christians have the same responsibility to maintain the holiness of
God's people that the Israelites did in the Old Testament. Given
Paul's strong reminders elsewhere that "All have sinned and fall
short of the glory of God," and more specifically that Paul himself
was "the worst of sinners,"[268] we know that our judgment of others
is not dependent on us first achieving a sinless state. We also see that
clear limits are set on who Christians are to judge—namely other

---

[267] Deuteronomy 17:7; 19:19; 21:21; 22:21, 24; 24:7.

[268] Romans 3:23; 1 Timothy 1:16.

professing believers who, despite the gentle restorative corrections from the body, continue to live in unrepentant sin.

Perhaps, like many folks, all this talk of discipline makes you uncomfortable because you have seen the untoward effects of misappropriated church discipline in your own life and in the lives of those around you. Maybe professing Christians have judged you on false standards or have been malicious toward you and rejoiced in your failures. If that is the case, then, on behalf of the body, I am truly sorry. Please know that this should never be. Discipline is necessary and healthy, but it is a process rife with pitfalls.

To discipline properly, we must keep the reference point straight. Our goal, as always, is to multiply God's rule in our own life and in the lives of those around us. Where others have gotten distracted and have wandered, we must lovingly and gently restore them that they might again experience the joyful reign of the King.

Distracted by Pride

If we are the person caught in sin, it is our responsibility to submit to the discipline of the church. While sin incites us to run from the harsh-seeming light of truth, we must stand our ground and trust that Jesus will indeed use this time of painful exposure to reveal lies that might be replaced with truth and so expand his kingdom rule in our hearts. If we reject the biblical rebukes of his body, then we also reject Christ.

Sadly, our first instinct is usually not toward humble reconciliation. Rather than running back to truth and life, our worldly reference point of pride tempts us to continue to choose death in order to save face. As it is written:

> *This is the verdict: Light has come into the world, but men loved darkness instead of light because their deeds were evil. Everyone who does evil hates the light, and will not come into the light for*

fear that his deeds will be exposed. But whoever lives by the truth comes into the light, so that it may be seen plainly that what he has done has been done through God.

—JOHN 3:19–21

Our tendency, as fallen humans, is to let the opinions of our fellow humans guide our approach to sin far more than any concern for the advancement of God's rule in our hearts. If the world says a particular sin is ugly and despicable, then we do, too. When that sin is our sin, we do not necessarily give it up, but we do make sure to bury it deep in the shadows of our lives and far from the scrutiny of our friends, family, and coworkers.

If our sin is acceptable to our world, or even to just our immediate peer group, then we tend to think very little of it. On the off chance that a Christian calls us out on such a sin, we revert to self-justification. Rather than simply admit to our deviation, we twist Jesus's clearest commandments up and down, left and right, until we find support for our decisions. If that does not work, we simply throw out the inflexible commandment as outdated and irrelevant.

In pride, many professing Christians have put themselves above the loving correction of Christ's Word and of his body. Without connection to the Vine, the faith they profess and maintain, in appearance, soon withers and dies. We should not let this be our story. Instead, we ought to bind ourselves to Christ's body: to bear and be borne, to sharpen and be sharpened, and to otherwise experience the beautiful, interdependent process of Christlike regeneration until the day we are re-created completely.

Distracted by Convenience

If we have managed to overcome the false reference point of worldly tolerance to speak boldly and consistently against the sin around us, it can be very tempting to want to stop there. Yet it is important to remember that sin often has physical consequences, too. Fornication, for example, can lead to disease, unwanted pregnancies, single parents, and child-support debt. Drunkenness can lead to loss of family, job, home, and health. Crime, whether it be driving without a license, tax evasion, or murder, can lead to fines, imprisonment, and lack of employability.

Because of these physical consequences, sin can have a measurable and long-lasting effect on the trajectory of our lives. Sometimes that effect can look like a physical blessing, as in Genesis when Abraham's and Isaac's lies regarding their wives led to them being paid off with money and possessions.[269] Surely no one would have any difficulty helping other sinners bear that kind of "burden," but what do we do when sin leads to the kind of ongoing hardships described in the previous paragraph? Consider asking yourself a few questions regarding your own experience:

- Do I listen to the world as it tells me to let others lie in the bed they have made for themselves, or do I set aside my convenience and my agenda to join in the struggles of my repentant brothers and sisters?
- Am I in moral proximity to physical and spiritual struggles, or have I passively placed myself at a distance from those folks with any substantial burdens? Has my local body done the same?

Robert Lupton, founder and president of FCS Urban Ministries, describes well the fear of coming together under such circumstances.

I fear contagion. I fear my life will get out of control, and I will be overwhelmed by the urgent affairs of others. I fear for my family. I resist Christ who beckons his followers to lay down their lives for each other. His talk of a yoke, a cross, of bearing one another's burdens and giving one's self away is not attractive to me. The implications of entering this world of suffering as a "Christ-one," as yeast absorbed

---

[269] Genesis 12:10–20; 20:1–18; 26:1–14.

*into the loaf of human need are as terrifying as death itself. Yet this
is the only way to life. The question is, will I choose life?*[270]

Life as a body gets messy when we take on the drama and upheaval
of others; there is no point in pretending otherwise. Are we willing
to bear one another up for the sake of the kingdom, regardless of
the burden, or will we, for convenience's sake, be content to be
spiritual consultants in this battle for all-of-life-encompassing
transformation?

A Kingdom-Centered Approach

*Whoever lives by the truth comes into the light, so that it may be
seen plainly that what he has done has been done through God.*

—JOHN 3:21

True disciples do not hide sin, whether it be our own or that of our
fellow believer, because sin undermines the rule of God, which we
have left everything to pursue. Rather than letting sin grow in the
shadows of our hearts, we confess it, that we might be healed and
filled all the more with Christ's rule.[271] Because sin is not simply
an issue between us and God, but between us and his body as well,
we confess before both God and his body. In Christ, we are light.
Though our remnant sinful nature fights to remain unknown in
darkness, we cannot. Ask yourself:

- When is the last time I confessed my sin to God or
  to others?
- Does my local church have a dedicated time for
  public confession of sin?

---

[270] Robert Lupton, *Theirs Is the Kingdom* (New York, NY: HarperCollins, 1989), 30.
[271] James 5:16.

- Do I justify my lack of confession because others
  have not experienced what I have gone through?[272]

After agreeing with God about the ugliness of our sin in confession, we must then completely reverse directions from chasing after sin to again pursuing God.[273] This change of direction is known as repentance, and without it our confession is proved insincere and our faith dead.[274] For the kingdom of heaven exists only in those who are submitting their *whole* lives—living, breathing, thinking, feeling, moving, and doing—to God's truth. There is simply no such thing as a talking but not walking Christian.

Even while confessing and repenting of our own sin, we need to be exhorting others to do the same. With unbelievers, the focus of our exhortations is on the worthiness of Christ as King, but with professing believers, our focus is on living out the rule of the King that is already claimed.

Remember that with our planks being continually removed and put to death, we are fit for rebuking, encouraging, and judging our brothers and sisters for God's glory and their joy. Our rebuke is always to be clothed in humility and gentleness—as one sinner to another—holding both of our lives up to the mutually-agreed-upon standard of God's Word.

When others have wronged us, we are to "forgive as the Lord has forgiven us."[275] To forgive someone means that we cancel his debt to us just as, in Christ, God has canceled our debt to him. We give up the right to be angry with others or harbor resentment against them. But this does not mean that life must go on as usual between us.

As we saw in the last chapter, there are times we ought to intentionally re-expose ourselves to potential injury and loss. There are also times that we ought to clearly and verbally demand change, as

---

[272] Others do not need to have first walked in our shoes to share in our walk because Christ walked in our shoes (Isaiah 53:3; Hebrews 4:15–16). Moreover, Christians all share the same Spirit and can minister to each other through him.

[273] Wood and Marshall, *Dictionary*, 1007.

[274] James 2:14–26.

[275] Colossians 3:13.

we saw earlier in the chapter with respect to church discipline.[276] The guiding purpose in every practical application of forgiveness is to spur both parties on toward godliness and a deeper love for the King.

Notice that forgiving others is our responsibility alone. When a person sins against us, we are called to forgive every time, regardless of circumstances. They may or may not confess, but we always forgive. They may or may not repent, but we forgive. We do so as many times as we are sinned against, just as Jesus taught his first disciples:

Then Peter came to Jesus and asked, "Lord, how many times shall I forgive my brother when he sins against me? Up to seven times?"

Jesus answered, "I tell you, not seven times, but seventy-seven times.

"Therefore, the kingdom of heaven is like a king who wanted to settle accounts with his servants. As he began the settlement, a man who owed him ten thousand talents was brought to him. Since he was not able to pay, the master ordered that he and his wife and his children and all that he had be sold to repay the debt.

"The servant fell on his knees before him. 'Be patient with me,' he begged, 'and I will pay back everything.' The servant's master took pity on him, canceled the debt, and let him go.

"But when that servant went out, he found one of his fellow servants who owed him a hundred denarii. He grabbed him and began to choke him. 'Pay back what you owe me!' he demanded.

---

[276] I imagine there could be an infinite number of possible changes to relationships. However, let me offer a few Scriptural principles to guide us through the ambiguity of such sad situations. First, we do not partner with unbelievers in any aspect of ministry, including marriage (2 Corinthians 6:14–18). Only in the case of marriage would we continue in an existing partnership in which our partner proves unfaithful to God (1 Corinthians 7:10–16). Second, we remove and exclude the unrepentant person from membership in our local body as a sign, to other believers and the world, of the spiritual reality behind un-teachability (1 Corinthians 5:1–13). Third, as long as they claim Christ yet live in willful sin, we continue to "gently instruct" them in truth, even after the local church has exercised its discipline (2 Timothy 2:25–26).

"His fellow servant fell to his knees and begged him, 'Be patient with me, and I will pay you back.'

"But he refused. Instead, he went off and had the man thrown into prison until he could pay the debt. When the other servants saw what had happened, they were greatly distressed and went and told their master everything that had happened.

"Then the master called the servant in. 'You wicked servant,' he said, 'I canceled all that debt of yours because you begged me to. Shouldn't you have had mercy on your fellow servant just as I had on you?' In anger his master turned him over to the jailers to be tortured, until he should pay back all he owed.

"This is how my heavenly Father will treat each of you unless you forgive your brother from your heart."

— MATTHEW 18:21–35

At least two truths are evident from Jesus's parable. First, our debt of sin against God is far worse than any debt of sin against us. We have no right to hold onto hate or anger when we have been forgiven for so much worse. Second, if we do not genuinely forgive others, then we have no place with God.[277]

It does not matter who sinned against us or what the particular sin was; we must forgive without exception. If we have been lied to, we must forgive the liar. If we have been robbed, we must forgive the thief. We must forgive again and again and again. Forgive our adulterous spouses. Forgive the drunk driver who killed our family members. Forgive our enemies. Forgive our abusers. The alternative is life without God.[278]

---

[277] As with every expression of godliness, forgiveness must come from the heart if it is to carry any hope of redemption. See Matthew 6:9–14 and Luke 11:2–4.

[278] Matthew 6:14; 18:35..

Let us now, as individuals, consider how we might add to the body's ability to bear with the sins of its members, our own sin included.

- What sin do I need to confess and repent? To whom will I confess it? What will a complete turnaround entail?
- Am I tolerating sin in others' lives? Why? Am I afraid that they would not receive rebuke well? Am I afraid that my own sin will be pointed out?
- Am I involved in Christlike discipleship that is committed to regular confession and, when necessary, rebuke?
- What did I do the last time someone asked me to deal with a particular sin in my life? Did I respond with repentance, or did I flee to another church?
- Am I willing to bear with others in their sin in all its ugliness, inconvenience, and drama? Will I give up leisure and rest to invest enough time in the lives of my fellow sinners that they may be borne up and restored?
- How far do people in my local church wander before I, or others in the church, recognize it and come alongside of them? What can I do to shorten that gap?[279]

This process of bearing with one another is incredibly hard. It requires letting down our guard and baring our souls openly before our fellow believers. We must come to them desiring to be known as we are, not as we think they wish us to be. Our souls must be laid bare, knowing that we are among sinners and will be hurt at times, but letting our desire to be refined overwhelm our instinct to hide.

---

[279] Scripture seems to indicate that bearing with one another only works when average Christians expect to be sharpened, trained, and encouraged in godliness by other average Christians. The top-heavy model of church that relies on a pastor and a handful of elders to do the majority of training in a church will simply not allow for the average member's struggles to be adequately cared for. Until we recover the biblical model of every-member discipleship, our efforts to bear with one another will be inconsistent and halfhearted, at best.

As members of one body in Christ, true believers cannot afford to merely struggle against our own sin; we must accept responsibility for the holiness of the body. When someone is tempted to withdraw into their sin, we make every effort to pull them back. We carry others in their struggle against sin even while they carry us. This is the only way to live in Christ.

15

A Perfect Unity

And over all these virtues put on love, which binds them all together in perfect unity. Let the peace of Christ rule in your hearts, since as members of one body you were called to peace. And be thankful.

—COLOSSIANS 3:14–15

preeminent love for God gives way to otherworldly, Christlike love for others that is compassionate, kind, humble, gentle, patient, and forgiving. While the world will often reject this kind of love, in the body of Christ it leads to the perfect unity that Jesus prayed for on behalf of his disciples. As the apostle John records:

My prayer is not for them alone. I pray also for those who will believe in me through their message, that all of them may be one, Father, just as you are in me and I am in you. May they also be in us so that the world may believe that you have sent me. I have given them the glory that you gave me, that they may be one as we

are one: I in them and you in me. May they be brought to complete
unity to let the world know that you sent me and have loved them
even as you have loved me.

—JOHN 17:20–23

With Christ as our collective head, no longer do we answer to the
earthly expectations of family, race, country, or ethnicity, for "here
there is no Greek or Jew, circumcised or uncircumcised, barbarian,
Scythian, slave or free, but Christ is all, and is in all."[280] Our hearts
and minds are fixed as one on his rule, and our diverse lives are
brought together in the unity of intimate proximity.

Nothing could be more obvious or tempting to a world of divisions and broken relationships than Christian unity,[281] which not
only flows from belief in the one true God of Scripture but also
bears witness to his character and our place in him. Praise the Lord
that there are local bodies of believers who model this well, both
in diverse membership and in their willing interactions with other
local bodies.

However, there is more work to be done. Sunday morning
worship services ought to bring folks from every tribe and nation
together in the name of Christ. Yet for many churches—even those
situated among diverse populations—Sunday remains the most
segregated time of the American week.

We have already explored how fear of stepping outside of our
socioeconomic and cultural assumptions has contributed to the
ongoing segregation among resourced and under-resourced. Let us
now look briefly at how our endless supply of Christian options
contributes to the disconnect between our unity of mind and our
practical separation from those who do not look, think, or talk like

---

[280] Colossians 3:11.

[281] Without the agreed-upon standard of a singular, preeminent Lord and Savior Jesus Christ, there is
no unity between believers and unbelievers. We still do our best to live at peace with the people of
this world, but we do so while waging relentless war on their gods (2 Corinthians 6:14–16).

us. After that, we will examine what it might look like to make every effort toward unity, as Scripture encourages us.

Distracted by Options

In our society, religions and denominations are like vendors in a marketplace, each vying for our business, which comes in the form of participation and charitable giving. Just like in a real marketplace, the customer is "king." This pressures local communities of faith to present a product that is, above all, appealing to its audience. Whether that product is true and healthy for the audience quickly becomes of lesser importance.

With the remnants of our old self still in the process of being put to death, we are still susceptible to the market dynamics of our religious landscape. Rather than seeking unity, we can be tempted to continue all manner of church start-ups and spin-offs until we have found one that is able to give us everything we want, while at the same time asking nothing of us that we are not willing to give. It is just as Paul warned Timothy:

The time will come when men will not put up with sound doctrine. Instead, to suit their own desires, they will gather around them a great number of teachers to say what their itching ears want to hear. They will turn their ears away from the truth and turn aside to myths.

— 2 TIMOTHY 4:3–4

Options are not inherently bad, but so often our choices are made without any active thought about what God desires for his church and us. We can waste years in a godless church, not growing or encouraging others to grow, because our family goes there, the people are friendly, the coffee is good, the music is familiar, or the pastor is well-known. The primary motivation for staying is our comfort, rather than furthering God's kingdom.

We can also waste years church hopping or shopping, looking for that perfect fit. In doing so, we never go deep enough among any one group of believers that we can be challenged and challenge others unto Christlikeness. This is a particular problem for young folks who can see finding the ideal church as part of the bigger process of breaking free from their parents' mold to find themselves. But it can also be a problem for older folks who fear having the order they worked so hard to achieve upset by needs or rebukes of others.

As one might expect with so many choices, we end up self-selecting into groups of people that think like us, talk like us, and worship like us. Theology-loving churches attract theology-loving people, service-oriented churches attract service-loving people, black churches attract black people, white churches attract white people, Indian churches attract Indian people, and so forth.

Sadly, Sunday afternoons and evenings in the fall and winter often offer a better approximation of unity than anything we do on Sunday mornings. It should devastate us to know that more folks from different races and backgrounds gather over their favorite football teams than they do for the "one God and Father of all."[282] Does it, though? Do we even notice?

Making Every Effort for Unity

Jesus's purpose in coming to earth was to "create in himself one new man out of the two, thus making peace, and in this one body to reconcile both of them to God through the cross, by which he put to death their hostility." Though we began as foreigners and aliens to each other, in Jesus, we are transformed into one people.

> *Therefore, remember that formerly you who are Gentiles by birth and called "uncircumcised" by those who call themselves "the circumcision" (that done in the body by the hands of men)— remember that at that time you were separate from Christ, excluded*

---

[282] Ephesians 4:6.

from citizenship in Israel and foreigners to the covenants of the promise, without hope and without God in the world. But now in Christ Jesus you who once were far away have been brought near through the blood of Christ.

For he himself is our peace, who has made the two one and has destroyed the barrier, the dividing wall of hostility, by abolishing in his flesh the law with its commandments and regulations. His purpose was to create in himself one new man out of the two, thus making peace, and in this one body to reconcile both of them to God through the cross, by which he put to death their hostility. He came and preached peace to you who were far away and peace to those who were near. For through him we both have access to the Father by one Spirit.

Consequently, you are no longer foreigners and aliens, but fellow citizens with God's people and members of God's household, built on the foundation of the apostles and prophets, with Christ Jesus himself as the chief cornerstone. In him the whole building is joined together and rises to become a holy temple in the Lord. And in him you too are being built together to become a dwelling in which God lives by his Spirit.

—*EPHESIANS 2:11–22*

Notice the language of diversity in proximity. People from every nation are brought, not only into one country, but into one household. Anyone who grew up in a large family or ever lived with a handful or more housemates can appreciate how close the walls of a house can bring individuals. While one could argue that this is all spiritual imagery, the example of the early church seems to affirm that our spiritual and physical realities are inextricably intertwined.

They devoted themselves to the apostles' teaching and to the fellowship, to the breaking of bread and to prayer. Everyone was filled with awe, and many wonders and miraculous signs were done by the apostles. All the believers were together and had everything in common. Selling their possessions and goods, they gave to anyone as he had need. Every day they continued to meet together in the temple courts. They broke bread in their homes and ate together with glad and sincere hearts, praising God and enjoying the favor of all the people. And the Lord added to their number daily those who were being saved.

—Acts 2:42–47

This kind of unity is hard to live out for even the most homogeneous of groups, but have we ever stopped to consider where "all the believers" in this passage came from? Does this not represent both those who followed Jesus while he walked the earth and the three thousand new converts drawn from the crowd at Pentecost made up of "Parthians, Medes, and Elamites; residents of Mesopotamia, Judea, and Cappadocia, Pontus and Asia, Phrygia and Pamphylia, Egypt and the parts of Libya near Cyrene; visitors from Rome (both Jews and converts to Judaism); Cretans and Arabs?"[283] These people did not even share the same language, and yet in Christ they were "together and had everything in common."

Certainly there is a danger of over-idealizing the early church, but this vision of diversity in proximate unity is not unrealistic in our day, nor is it optional. While social, geographical, economic, and cultural reference points pull us apart, Christ demands that we live life together and minister hand-in-hand with one another as a testimony of his preeminent worthiness. While we need not all live in the same house, we ought to gladly seek out each other's company, both in public and in private.

At the very least, we are to reflect the diversity of our communities. However, given that socioeconomic values and opportunities rather than godly ones largely decide the makeup of our communities, we may have to consider relocating ourselves to achieve

---

[283] Acts 2:9–11.

Christlike unity. This will not be easy. It will take a complete paradigm shift, in which kingdom advancement is given priority over our deeply ingrained cultural assumptions and earthly common sense.

Praise the Lord that small pockets of his people are already experiencing that paradigm shift and spreading out across our country and around the world. The "haves" are joining hands with the "have-nots." Red and yellow, black and white are doing life together in spite of personal and societal inertia that would keep them apart. As they do so, some of the early church's otherworldly, Christlike presence is being recovered.

Getting different people together, however, is only the first step toward Christlike unity. The tendency is always to separate out again. We do not need to be racist or hateful. We need only to continue to follow our thoroughly practical yet broken instincts toward whatever brings the most comfort and convenience at the least cost to us. Like oil from water, the separation is effortless, leaving the young singles over in one corner, the folks who are married with kids in another, blue-collar here, and white-collar over there.

To avoid separation, we must be constantly remixing and reintegrating ourselves, all the while inviting new folks in to experience God in the words and deeds of his body. This is what it means for believers to make every effort "to keep the unity of the Spirit" and "to do what leads to peace and mutual edification."[284]

What about you and me, though? Are we constantly remixing and reintegrating ourselves? Does unity in the body of Christ motivate our everyday decisions about whom to work, play, live, and worship alongside? Consider the following questions as you measure your efforts toward unity in the body of Christ:

- Do I share God's intense passion for unity in his body, or do I make excuses for the church's segregation?

---

[284] Ephesians 4:3; Romans 14:19.

- Am I contributing to the unity of the body or to the world's status quo? What will it take for me to change?
- Am I willing to go beyond friendships and let the call to unity lead to more costly strategies like relocation and redistribution?
- What would it take for me to commit to living and working and playing and worshiping alongside of brothers and sisters who do not look or speak like me, even when it hurts?

Recovering the unity of Christ within a local body is important; however, another level of unity—*between* local bodies of believers—is also worth considering. Because of our marketplace mentality with religion, local churches are almost as diverse as individuals in their beliefs and worship styles. Their differences represent both an obstacle to and an opportunity for unity and balance within the body. To illustrate this point, let us look briefly at the prototypical variation among the seven churches described in Revelation 2–3:

- *Sardis.* From the outside, the church at Sardis looked very much alive. But they had wandered from God's truth. Despite their flurry of activities, they had forgotten the truth of the gospel and how to live it out. Without truth, their deeds were incomplete and meaningless. Do our churches offer numerous activities without pointing anyone to Jesus? Do we have dozens of ministries but few believers who observe and pass on the Lord's teachings?
- *Laodicea.* Here is another church that Jesus had nothing good to say about. Their earthly wealth had left them self-satisfied, with no appetite for the riches of God. Moreover, they identified so much with the spiritual temperature of the world around

them that they were said to be lukewarm, neither hot nor cold. Are our churches likewise filled with resourced people who do not want to be bothered with the day-to-day grind of ministry? Is life on earth so good, comfortable, or secure that we no longer ache for Jesus's return?

- *Philadelphia and Smyrna.* These are the only churches for whom Jesus had nothing but encouragement. He talked to them tenderly, recognizing their weakness and poverty, and praising their perseverance in the truth of the gospel. All these churches had was faithfulness in the face of afflictions—nothing else on earth to encourage them. But their eyes were not fixed on what was seen; rather they were fixed on the unseen King. Do our churches also faithfully hold onto the gospel of Jesus? All of it? Are we persecuted because of it?

- *Pergamum.* Like Philadelphia and Smyrna, Pergamum endured intense persecution. Yet unlike those two churches, Pergamum did not hold firm to the gospel by preserving its absolute and exclusive claims. While they held onto Jesus, they also made the grievous error of accepting false teachers and idolatry and sexual immorality. Jesus was good and real and worth being persecuted for, but in their minds, holiness and doctrine were not. Do our churches preach the need for repentance and a forgiveness of sins?[285] Or is Jesus just a friend, always affirming and never rebuking? Is Jesus the only way to God, or one of many viable options?

- *Ephesus.* Unlike Pergamum, Ephesus knew exactly what to do with false teachers. They were a doctrinally sound church that had no tolerance for those

---

[285] Luke 24:45–48.

who claimed a Jesus other than the one who is described in the gospels. Do our churches cultivate a passion for preserving truth and exposing the heresies of our day? Praise the Lord! We must be faithful in preserving sound doctrine. But the Ephesians had forgotten how to love God and others with their deeds. Do our churches regularly enforce discipline without putting in the time and effort to walk with people before they fall into grievous sin? Are calls for justice and mercy made from our pulpits? Do they find their ways into our budgets? Are we teaching people to love in word and deed?

- *Thyatira.* This church modeled the deeds of faith well. They loved and served with increasing passion. Maybe our churches do well with that, too—feeding the hungry, clothing the naked, visiting the prisoner, and righting injustices. If so, praise the Lord, but do not miss the rebuke. In their efforts to be loving, the Thyatirans had tolerated idolatry, sexual immorality, and false doctrine in their local body. Are our churches likewise so caught up in doing the things Jesus did that we forget to also say the things he said? Do we discipline those who, though they claim to follow Christ, are living in unrepentant sin?

One of the things we ought to take away from these examples is the desire to challenge our local body of believers to balanced kingdom building. This is for everyone, whether we are the pastor or the person who always sits in the back row. Imbalanced churches are called to repent in the same way as those churches that got nothing right at all. None of us, as Christians, can afford to sit by while our churches pigeonhole the gospel—specializing in part at the expense of the whole.

Sadly, by self-selecting our way into bodies of believers, we tend to magnify our weaknesses by surrounding ourselves with similarly imbalanced folks. Given enough time, we begin to justify the neglect of our now-common weaknesses by questioning the need for those attributes at all. For example, if we are strong in doctrine, we are liable to belittle the need for justice and mercy, openly questioning the faith of those who make such things a priority. We call them liberals and assume they have no sense of what truly matters in life. In contrast, if we are passionate for justice and mercy and compassion, we will often respond by making everyone else out to be self-righteous, heartless Pharisees.

Why do we do this? Are we so insecure in our faith that we must bolster ourselves at the expense of others? Why not, instead, learn from the strengths of other churches, while offering to admonish them from our strengths (if we have any)? Why not have strong doctrinal churches, like Ephesus; seek out churches that do a great job of loving their neighbors, like Thyatira? And why not have service-oriented churches enlist the help of doctrinally oriented churches to keep them on the straight and narrow? Finally, why not have churches who are in danger of letting their wealth lull them to sleep, like the Laodiceans, give away their earthly treasures, both to alleviate the suffering of churches like Smyrna and to discover what true treasure looks like?[286]

Seeking first the kingdom through the unity of its people is essential and it is messy. As sinners among sinners, the closer we get to each other, the more we can expect our brokenness to be exposed. Yet, this messiness is light and momentary next to the eternal delight of being in Christ. So let us take an honest look at our lives and intentionally make decisions that increase our ability to cultivate and encourage the unity of the body, for God's glory and our joy.

---

[286] One of my favorite examples of diverse churches coming together in the name of Jesus Christ for mutual sharpening is the International Congress on World Evangelization that took place at Lausanne in 1974. Believers from over 150 nations came together to discuss how to go about fulfilling our common call to "make disciples of every nation." Together, they drafted a fifteen-point document known as the Lausanne Covenant that continues to provide a brief yet balanced look at the fundamental truths that define our default mission as Christians. I encourage you to read the covenant for yourself at http://www.lausanne.org/en/documents/lausanne-covenant.html.

IV
Life *for* Christ

Let the word of Christ dwell in you richly as you teach and admonish one another with all wisdom, and as you sing psalms, hymns and spiritual songs with gratitude in your hearts to God. And whatever you do, whether in word or deed, do it all in the name of the Lord Jesus, giving thanks to God the Father through him.

—COLOSSIANS 3:16–17

16

From Grace to Thanks

Let the word of Christ dwell in you richly as you teach and admonish one another with all wisdom, and as you sing psalms, hymns and spiritual songs with gratitude in your hearts to God. And whatever you do, whether in word or deed, do it all in the name of the Lord Jesus, giving thanks to God the Father through him.

—COLOSSIANS 3:16–17

We are now in the final stretch of our passage from Colossians. Having taught us to set our hearts and minds on the reign of Christ, to put to death all of our idolatrous distractions, and to put on all of Christ, Paul now takes a step back. The details are left to consider again our common call as Christians to seek first the kingdom above by choosing to do "whatever" we do for the Lord Jesus. We will look at this choice in the next chapter, but first I want to examine the motivation behind it, which is grace.

Our attitude in Christ stands in sharp contrast to the anger that results from our old self's disappointed expectations—both getting the bad things we feel we *do not* deserve and failing to get the good things that we feel we *do* deserve. Now, as re-created beings with the Spirit of God inside of us, we are freed to see his hand working out each detail of our life—regardless of appearance—for our good. Thankfulness flows, quite naturally, from the reality of our expectations being perpetually exceeded.

We are like a sixteen-year-old at Christmas who, instead of receiving socks as he expected, was just given the keys to a brand-new car. Imagine how overwhelming such a gift would be. After thanking his parents profusely, could his thankfulness help but overflow in the constant retelling of the story of their gift to his friends and to everyone else who noticed his new car?

So it is for those who have accepted the free and undeserved gift of our triune God. Only one response is possible: a life welling up and spilling over with thankfulness. As Paul wrote earlier in his letter to the Colossians:

> *So then, just as you received Christ Jesus as Lord, continue to live in him, rooted and built up in him, strengthened in the faith as you were taught, and overflowing with thankfulness.*

> —COLOSSIANS 2:6–7

In an exhortation to the believers in Rome, Paul again highlights our proper response to God's grace:

> *Therefore, I urge you, brothers, in view of God's mercy, to offer your bodies as living sacrifices, holy and pleasing to God—this is your spiritual act of worship.*

> —ROMANS 12:1

Because God has promised to work out everything for our good, we are able (and commanded) to be thankful in all circumstances, whether things turn out the way we want them to or not. As Paul writes to the Thessalonians:

> *Be joyful always; pray continually; give thanks in all circumstances, for this is God's will for you in Christ Jesus.*

> — *1 Thessalonians 5:16–18*

The command to "be joyful always" forces us to take a hard look at our lives and let God redefine our sense of good. Frustrations, disappointments, trials, and persecutions will come, not in spite of God, but because of him.[287] He gives us these seemingly bad things, yet at the very same time demands thankfulness so that we might be forced to stop and consider the glorious and weighty good that stands behind every circumstance for those who love God.[288]

Thus, we are not merely thankful *in* every circumstance. We are thankful *for* every circumstance. How else would we receive God's good and perfect gift? The superficially bad things (that we all experience to some degree) serve as constant reminders of this world's sinful and fractured state, desperately in need of re-creation. Trials and struggles are catalysts for believers' eager anticipation, hope, and thankfulness for that day when all things will be made new.[289]

As Paul told the Romans, our thankfulness leads to us offering ourselves as living sacrifices that bring Christ glory by bearing his image. We cultivate godliness through frequent prayer, careful study of God's Word, and regular sharpening at the hands of our discipler and the community of disciples at large. As we do so, and our minds are renewed, we are able to root out, cast down, and put to death our idols. We are also able to finally put on Christ, not

---

[287] Ecclesiastes 7:14, Isaiah 45:7.

[288] Romans 8:28.

[289] Romans 8:18–25; Revelation 21:1–8.

in some abstract reality, but in everyday life, by adopting his otherworldly values and lifestyle of compassion, kindness, humility, gentleness, patience, forgiveness, and love.

Spurred on by our thankfulness, we are free to choose whatever details—the who, where, what, how, and when—so long as those details further encourage us to fulfill our created purpose.[290] Remember, we have been set free for Jesus Christ, to extend his rule by bearing his image in word and deed. He does not care about the specific details of life so long as they are chosen for his glory.

Our response to God's grace can easily be misdirected if we fail to understand the nature of our freedom in Christ. In particular, there are two false reference points—legalism or licentiousness—that can keep us from living a life overflowing with grace-motivated thankfulness. These reference points pass themselves off as true kingdom living but only serve to distract us from the straight and narrow path of singular devotion to God. They are dangerous enough and common enough that we will do well to examine them here before moving on to a discussion of the grace-motivated life.

Distracted by Legalism

In legalism, we struggle to believe that we are free from the law and that our status in Christ does not somehow depend on our actions. So we take the focus off of Jesus and put it on his commands. Though the shift may seem subtle, the result is the idolatry of self-righteousness. As J. I. Packer writes:

Legalism is a distortion of obedience that can never produce truly good works. Its first fault is that it skews motive and purpose, seeing good deeds as essentially ways to earn more of God's favor than one has at the moment. Its second fault is arrogance. Belief that one's labor earns God's favor begets contempt for those who do

---

[290] There is no one right career or spouse (if any) or school or neighborhood that we have to find to please Christ. But we do have to be honest with ourselves about what it means practically to give God first priority in our lives and to encourage his preeminence in the hearts and lives of those around us.

not labor in the same way. Its third fault is lovelessness in that its self-advancing purpose squeezes humble kindness and creative compassion out of the heart.[291]

We may be tempted to, like the Pharisees of Jesus's time, imagine that our morality saves us apart from God. In that case we do not need a sacrifice, because we have overcome our own sin. We may also, like the Judaizers of Paul's time, attempt to add something onto the gospel to complete it. The latter situation is a much subtler form of legalism that caused even the apostle Peter to compromise the gospel for a time.[292] Paul's reminder to believers who struggle with legalism is simple.

It is for freedom that Christ has set us free. Stand firm, then, and do not let yourselves be burdened again by a yoke of slavery.

—*GALATIANS 5:1*

We are to stand firm in the reality of our freedom. As believers, we are no longer under the law because through Jesus we fulfill it. When we yield to Christ's reign in our lives, he gives us the Holy Spirit to dwell in us, and as we yield to the Holy Spirit, he fills us with more and more of his desires. While these desires invariably lead us to bear Jesus's image in its entirety and to build his kingdom, we are free to do that in our own rhythm and flavor.

Freedom from the law, in a sense, takes away the script and forces us to make our own decisions. At the same time, it gives others room to make different decisions that lead to different-looking lives. This does not mean we cannot hold other Christians accountable to the clear commands of Scripture, including the preeminent pursuit of the kingdom, but we must resist the urge to add onto the

---

[291] *Concise Theology.*

[292] See Galatians 2:11–3:3. Judaizers were folks who told non-Jewish believers that in addition to believing in and living for Jesus Christ, they also had to adhere to the old Jewish laws to be saved.

words of Christ. He did not free folks just for us to tie them back down with our standards for holy living.

A good friend of mine uses the example of drinking alcohol to illustrate how we extend our practical wisdom into godly requirements of others. While the Bible condemns drunkenness, it never condemns drinking alcohol in moderation. In turning water into wine, you could even argue that Jesus implicitly approves of social drinking that does not lead to drunkenness. Still, without Scripture's backing, believers have been and continue to be tempted to prohibit others from drinking.

Most often this desire to prohibit is motivated by the practical and experiential wisdom that comes from seeing the great evil of drunkenness and the havoc that it has wrought in so many lives. There is nothing wrong with this kind of compassion, but it should never lead us to say, "Do not handle! Do not taste! Do not touch!"[293] because God does not place those commands on us. We may appeal to practical wisdom, particularly in the case of a recovering alcoholic, but we cannot make abstinence from alcohol a condition of righteousness.

Again, where Christ is silent, we must not put words in his mouth. Like it or not, there are gray areas in Scripture. Not every decision is black-and-white. It is good to hold specific convictions based on general principles. But we cannot demand the same convictions of others. So long as others are putting Christ first in their lives, we should be applauding their efforts. Consider the following questions as you explore your tendencies toward legalism:

- Do I believe success in life is always deserved and earned?
- Do I seek to gain approval of others by acting a certain way or by performing at a certain level?

---

[293] Colossians 2:21. Paul goes on to say in Colossians 2:22–23, "These are all destined to perish with use, because they are based on human commands and teachings. Such regulations indeed have an appearance of wisdom, with their self-imposed worship, their false humility, and their harsh treatment of the body, but they lack any value in restraining sensual indulgence."

- Do I believe that how I pray, either in quality or quantity, effects God's willingness to respond? In other words, do I think I can force his hand?
- Do I insist that others adhere to my preferences along with Scripture's principles?

Distracted by Licentiousness

The second false reference point that we are liable to fall for is licentiousness. This is the abuse of freedom, as a license to do whatever our earthly nature pleases, and honestly, this is where many of us live. We open the door to Jesus just enough for him to shove his blessings in. He becomes the perfect combination of a genie and a fire insurance policy—a better way to get what we already wanted on earth without the having to worry about going to hell when it is all over.

However comforting to our self-absorbed lives this god may be, he is not the Jesus of Scripture for whom faith and obedience are inseparable. We may have been freed from the penalty of the law, through Jesus's sacrifice as believers, but it still has an ongoing role in our lives. To those who would persist in licentiousness Paul says:

You, my brothers, were called to be free. But do not use your freedom to indulge the sinful nature; rather, serve one another in love.

—GALATIANS 5:13

Paul makes it clear that the freedom we enjoy is the freedom to love one another, without trying to earn God's favor, and that in loving others we fulfill the very law used to condemn us.

Let no debt remain outstanding, except the continuing debt to love one another, for he who loves his fellowman has fulfilled the law. The commandments, "Do not commit adultery," "Do not murder," "Do not steal," "Do not covet," and whatever other commandment there may be, are summed up in this one rule: "Love your neighbor as yourself." Love does no harm to its neighbor. Therefore love is the fulfillment of the law.

—ROMANS 13:8–10

While we do not add onto Scripture, we do not take away from it either. Where Scripture is firm, we, too, must stand resolutely. Sound doctrine is crucial and must be defended. As Christians, we are free to do whatever we do to the glory of God, but we are not free to do whatever we want, because we still have old-self desires waging war inside of us. Not everything we want to do or can do in this life is of benefit to the kingdom. Many things are quite the opposite, undermining Jesus's rule by gratifying the other gods we are juggling.

The freedom Christ offers is freedom from the desires of our sinful nature and the just punishment that serving those desires has earned us. In Christ, our sinful nature no longer controls us and renders us incapable of pursuing God. We are freed, through the power of the Holy Spirit who now lives in us, to rediscover and appease our created appetite for the righteousness of God.

A Grace-Motivated Overflow of Thanks

The proper motivation for kingdom-first discipleship, and the one that guards against these last two false reference points, is the overwhelming and undeserved favor of God that was poured out on us in creation and all the more clearly in re-creation. Such grace ought to inspire in us the humility and gratitude necessary for binding our wandering hearts to our King.

Humility comes from realizing that we were dead in our transgressions, unable and unwilling to be reconciled to God. It keeps us from trying to earn God's favor and drives us to throw ourselves repeatedly on mercy of God. Gratitude comes from knowing that God loved us, his enemies, so much that he willingly laid down his life to pay for our sins. It keeps us from abusing our freedom.

Yet God's grace does not merely keep us from sin. His unmerited favor in our lives inspires profound gratitude, which wells up and overflows in many thanks. We become living sacrifices of praise, with every part of our existence—how we think, how we act, and how we speak—rediscovering its role in thanking God for his goodness and enduring love.[294]

While any talk of sacrifice is likely to be received with fear, that should not be the case when it comes to God. To the contrary, God's grace makes this a wonderfully exciting proposition because Jesus offers us the great reward in exchange for our sinful brokenness. He takes our trash and gives us treasure. What wondrous love and mercy! No room is left for defending or clinging to our earthly idols, only the delight of looking on the one true God.

So much of this book has been devoted to what it looks like, in terms of deeds, to live life as a child of the King. That has been intentional because it is always easier to talk a good talk than to walk in the footsteps of Christ. At the same time, do not miss the necessity of giving voice to our thanks. Thankfulness *looks* like putting off sin and putting on Christ and it *sounds* like songs, prayers, and the retelling of God's story. As Paul wrote:

> *And be thankful. Let the word of Christ dwell in you richly as you teach and admonish one another with all wisdom, and as you sing psalms, hymns and spiritual songs with gratitude in your hearts to God.*

> —COLOSSIANS 3:15–16

Whether we feel gifted or called to music or evangelism is irrelevant. Everyone is to audibly give testimony to God's graciousness, in both song and conversation. For many Christians this comes effortlessly, like the sixteen-year-old who was given a car instead of socks for Christmas. For others, however, especially those who have known

---

[294] Jeremiah 33:10–11.

Christ for years and grown comfortable in their knowledge, bearing testimony to the worthiness of God takes much more effort. The problem is, without constant refreshment, the reality of God's goodness fades with time and so does our tangible delight.

To use myself as an example, evangelism is neither my nature nor my gift. Rarely, if ever, am I inclined to strike up conversations with complete strangers. Even among friends, I tend to avoid things that make me look foolish or create awkwardness in a conversation, and can always whip up a dozen reasons why any given circumstance is not ideal to sharing the good news of what Christ has done in my life. However, considering what God has done and continues to do for me, my personality and other excuses prove to be nothing more than thinly veiled ingratitude and spite. Jesus's words to his disciples expose my heart, crippled as it is by pride.

If anyone is ashamed of me and my words in this adulterous and sinful generation, the Son of Man will be ashamed of him when he comes in his Father's glory with the holy angels.

—MARK 8:38

What about you? Are you silent and ashamed in your everyday life or are you thankful? Consider asking yourself the following questions:

- When was the last time I told an unbeliever about God's good work in my life or in the life of his people throughout history?[295]
- Am I willing to be considered a fool for praising God openly, or to be cast aside by my friends for being too exclusive and unnecessarily concerned with one thing?

---

[295] This is not a contest. The point is not is not so much whether it was five minutes ago or five weeks ago, so long as we are regularly and frequently seeking out, and even orchestrating, opportunities to share the gospel with others.

Giving thanks to God out loud is simply to tell of his goodness in our lives. It is our testimony, or story, of God's hand at work in our hearts and circumstances. As we renew our minds with Scripture, we will find that we have more to thank God for: his righteousness, miraculous works, redemption from sin, the wisdom and power to serve him, and the faith and love of others.

Whether life seems pleasant or not, we know that God is working it out for the good of those who love him. So we ought to thank him privately and publicly, with our voices and with instruments,[296] and we should proclaim our gratitude for his love before the assembly of believers and before the nations.[297] In everything, our thankfulness should be an intentional and joyful expression of worship to our great and loving God.

---

[296] 1 Chronicles 25:3.

[297] 2 Samuel 22:50, Psalm 35:18; Psalm 105:1, Isaiah 12:4.

17

The Choice

And whatever you do, whether in word or deed, do it all in the name of the Lord Jesus, giving thanks to God the Father through him.

—COLOSSIANS 3:17

At first glance it may seem that this verse is an encouragement to find ways of bringing God glory through whatever we are already doing or already want to do. For instance, if we are an engineer, we may try to apply this verse by becoming a friendlier, better educated engineer, who complains less than our coworkers and shares Christ with them over lunch, and uses our "gift" to serve the needy by digging wells or building homes in third-world countries. While those certainly sound like good and noble things to do, Christianizing our existing lives is not Paul's aim.

The command to do "whatever we do...in the name of the Lord Jesus" assumes that we have already died to the old self and been re-created in Christ, with the Holy Spirit birthing new kingdom-first desires in our hearts. This represents a complete break from our previous self-centered existence, regardless of how morally we lived or talented we were in worldly terms. Thus, "whatever we do" should not be carried over thoughtlessly from our previous life, but rather, intentionally chosen according to its effect on our own godliness (i.e., image bearing) and our ability to encourage God's rule in those around us.

Death and Emptying

Most professing Christians today are not bowing down to graven images with any regularity. However, as we have seen, this does not mean that we are not idolaters. Nor does the fact that we give lip service to Jesus mean that he is our King. So often we come to Christ with the hope of adding him on to our already full lives. We then spend our time trying to find the perfect "balance" between the demands of Jesus and the obligations, values, and assumptions related to our family and friends, jobs, dreams, talents, locations, hobbies, housing situations, and local church bodies.

But treating Jesus as a god among gods will not save us. He must be our all, which means every part of our old lives, including the good things and the seemingly indispensable *have-tos,* must be placed on the chopping block, ready to be cut off if need be to preserve our singular eye for the King. As Dietrich Bonhoeffer wrote:

> *The life of discipleship can only be maintained so long as nothing is allowed to come between Christ and ourselves—neither the law, nor personal piety, nor even the world. The disciple always looks only to his master, never to Christ and the law, Christ and religion, Christ and the world. He avoids all such notions like the plague. Only by following Christ alone can he preserve the single eye. His eye rests wholly on the light that comes from Christ, and has no darkness or ambiguity in it.*[298]

---

[298] Bonhoeffer, *Discipleship*, 173.

Consider the following questions to help with determining what in your life needs to go:

- Am I currently living in unconfessed and willful sin? How can I put that to death?
- What are the top five things I spend God's time, talent, and resources on? Are these things adding to my witness or distracting from it? Are these things an end in themselves, or are they a means of, directly or indirectly, furthering God's kingdom?
- What situations or people tempt me to make an idol of sex, money, or earthly life, liberty, and the pursuit of happiness?
- What would prevent me from going all in and rearranging my whole life for the kingdom?
- What is my life building toward? What do I want to be known for? Have I put a good thing in God's place on the throne of my heart?

The process of kingdom-first transformation will be costly, and at first we will feel pulled in a thousand directions as the chains between our hearts and our idols are stretched tight and finally broken. The fact that this process hurts should not surprise us or cause us to question our decision to follow Christ. Emptying ourselves of ourselves requires putting our earthly nature to death on the cross of Christ. Though painful, nothing could be more normal to the believer's experience.

The cross is laid on every Christian. The first Christ-suffering, which every man must experience, is the call to abandon the attachments of this world. It is that dying of the old man which is the result of the first encounter with Christ. As we embark upon discipleship, we surrender ourselves to Christ in union with his death—we give over our lives to death. Thus it begins; the cross is not the terrible end to an otherwise god-fearing and happy life, but it meets us at the beginning of communion with Christ. When Christ calls a man, he bids him come and die.[299]

Life Filled with Christ

Death is not where our story ends. That is only the beginning. Jesus was crucified and resurrected so that we might also pass from death to life and from cross to throne. As Jesus explained to the first disciples:

If anyone would come after me, he must deny himself and take up his cross daily and follow me. For whoever wants to save his life will lose it, but whoever loses his life for me will save it. What good is it for a man to gain the whole world, and yet lose or forfeit his very self?

—*LUKE 9:23–25*

This seemingly paradoxical promise of Jesus is that in living for ourselves, we end up dying, but in dying to ourselves and living for him, we find the very thing we thought we gave up, and more. He came that we "may have life, and have it to the full" *in* him, starting today and stretching for eternity.[300]

Life in Christ is a progressive and intentional rediscovery of our created purpose to bear the image of our Creator. Together we have looked at a few aspects of Christ's image: love, compassion, kindness, humility, gentleness, patience, forgiveness, and peace. This list is not exhaustive, but it is a good place to start. We could have easily extended it to include other attributes of God such as justice, mercy, joy, faithfulness, and self-control.

As we seek to grow in Christlikeness, we must carefully weigh our everyday decisions (e.g., what we eat, drink, or wear or who we spend our time with or where we live) for their effect on our ability and desire to bear God's image. Few if any decisions are truly neutral in this respect. Thus, it is appropriate that we as individuals

---

[299] Bonhoeffer, *Discipleship*, 89.
[300] John 10:10.

soberly examine our lives for those elements or situations in life that encourage us, with our unique blend of spiritual strengths and weaknesses, to put on Christ in all his otherworldly glory. Consider the following questions for yourself:

- What are the things (or who are the people) that make me want to treasure Jesus more? Do I need more of these in my life?
- Am I currently making use of Scripture, prayer, discipleship, and fellowship to encourage my own godliness? What circumstances increase my ability or desire to put them to use?[301]
- Where have I already begun to put on Christlike love as demonstrated in otherworldly compassion, kindness, humility, gentleness, patience, and forgiveness?
- What areas of godliness are weak or nonexistent in my day-to-day life? How can I arrange the details of my life—who, what, where, how, and when—to challenge me to growth in these areas?

Our source of godliness is the Holy Spirit. Through his power we are to strive to put on all of Christ. Having come so far, we cannot afford to settle for half gods or half gospels at this point. While our fallen tendency is to make much of those attributes of Christ that come easiest to us and neglect the rest, that is not how the Spirit works within true believers. He bears his whole character in every believer in the form of common fruit.

The fact that we are all bearing the same fruit does not mean we are all to be living the same lives, in the same places, with the same mix of details. For while we share one Lord and one faith and one calling, we nevertheless have different temperaments, natural strengths and weaknesses, spiritual gifts and outages, educational backgrounds, and socioeconomic capital. Because of that, we may each require a unique mix of location, relationships, careers,

---

[301] See appendices 2, 3, and 4 for more discussion of these kingdom building tools.

recreational activities, education, and family to spur us on in our pursuit of the kingdom.

Multiplying

Individual image bearing is not an end in itself. It never has been. As we saw in creation, image bearers have always been expected to reproduce themselves in others. In a de-created world, the call remains. We who have been re-created in Christ become his light, the very righteousness of God, shining forth in midst of the kingdom of darkness. We become ambassadors and agents of reconciliation among all the peoples of the earth as God makes his appeal through our words and deeds.[302]

God's design for our multiplication through reconciliation, is to be disciples who make disciples of all nations. This is not optional, or extra-credit, Christianity. Nor are the basic elements of discipleship up for debate. As Jesus's parting instructions remind us, discipleship means going, baptizing, and teaching.[303]

All authority in heaven and on earth has been given to me. Therefore go and make disciples of all nations, baptizing them in the name of the Father and of the Son and of the Holy Spirit, and teaching them to obey everything I have commanded you. And surely I am with you always, to the very end of the age.

—MATTHEW 28:18–20

"Going" is the first part of the command to make disciples. It is more assumed than asserted in the passage in Matthew. The sense in the passage is "as you are going," be making disciples. This again sounds very similar to the language of Deuteronomy 6:4-9 where God's people are to be impressing love for God on their children whether at home or on the road, lying down or getting up. Every part of our lives is an opportunity to image God in word or deed.

---

[302] 2 Corinthians 5:17–21.

[303] For more on discipleship see appendix 4.

The purpose of going is to put ourselves in position to meet the spiritual and physical needs of our world. We do not have to wait around for a vision or audible voice or any other specialized call from God on our lives, because he has shown us who he is and what he is about. Where God's kingdom is undermanned or under-armed, we mobilize people and resources (ourselves and our own included) to meet that need.

Deciding when and where we go should include a sober evaluation of our spiritual strengths and weaknesses and our level of maturation in Christ. Trusted Christians should be sought to confirm our self-assessment; then the options can be weighed. What situations allow us to use our strengths while at the same challenging us to grow in our weaknesses? Are we infants in the faith, liable to be tossed around by whatever teachings we are around, or are we rooted firm in Christ, ready to start affecting those around us in his name?

If we are new to the faith or discipleship, then our initial steps should be toward finding a biblically sound, local body of believers who exhibit well-balanced image bearing. Before we make disciples, we must learn for ourselves what Christ taught and what it looks like to live under his rule. On the other hand, those who are already rooted and built up in the faith should begin to measure decisions increasingly by how each choice allows them to cultivate God's rule in the hearts of those around them.

While going, we are also to be baptizing. This is the second part of the command to make disciples, and it usually brings to mind the image of someone being immersed (or sprinkled) with water. In a larger sense, however, baptism symbolizes initiation into the fold of God's people much the way circumcision did for the Jews of the Old Testament. If we forget this larger context, we are liable to neglect the assumptions underlying the rite of baptism—namely that God's people are seeking out opportunities for invitation and witness.

Nonbelievers ought to be able to experience God in his Word and in the life of his people. This task of invitation and initiation is what we commonly refer to as evangelism. It is not separate from making disciples, as we often speak of it, but an integral part of building God's kingdom from outside of its current boundaries.[304] By nature, initiation into God's fold requires going out into the kingdom of darkness to bring wandering sinners back under the rule of God.[305]

Finally, along with going out and baptizing, we are also to be teaching. In contrast to baptizing, where we are inviting new members into the body of Christ, teaching means building up those who are already under God's rule. This is the task we commonly refer to as discipleship, and the goal is to train our disciples to fix their eyes solely on King Jesus and let his seemingly upside-down values become the assumptions that frame their thinking.[306] Where there is sin, it is put to death. Where good deeds are lacking, we push our disciples toward tangible expression of their singular love.

Obedience to God's will of desire is how the internal, invisible kingdom is made manifest to the world around us. The Holy Spirit indwells believers, changing them from the inside out. His character is revealed in the disciple's interactions with the world. Image bearing is not theological theory; it is our life. We do not give mere lip service to love, faith, or justice, lest we forfeit the credibility of our message. Rather we lay down our lives to make God's otherworldly character a tangible reality for our neighbor.[307]

Healthy believers bear fruit and multiply. Our goal in making disciples is to bring nonbelievers into the fold of God and build them up to a point where they can reiterate the basic truths of the faith as well as live them out, eventually using both word and deed to multiply their faith in others.

---

[304] Romans 10:14–15.

[305] Luke 15:3–7.

[306] God's kingdom comes with many unintuitive values. For example, leaders serve and servants lead (Mark 10:41–45); the foolish are chosen to shame the wise (1 Corinthians 1:27); and greatness is measured by putting God's commands into practice and teaching others to do the same (Matthew 5:19). For more examples of upside-down values, read the beatitudes in Matthew 5:3–12.

[307] 1 John 4:12.

A Final Call

This day I call heaven and earth as witnesses against you that I have set before you life and death, blessings and curses. Now choose life, so that you and your children may live and that you may love the Lord your God, listen to his voice, and hold fast to him. For the Lord is your life.

—DEUTERONOMY 30:19–20

We have come a long way together. Thank you for joining me. My hope was to provide a practical look at the essentials of right thinking and right living that make up the default mode of operation of a true Christian. When confronted with God's truth, we can choose to do life his way, which will require a dramatic restructuring of our self-first lives into kingdom-first lives, or we can choose to go on doing it our way. Doing things God's way leads to life, whereas doing it our way means death and suffering.

If we take up our cross and follow Jesus in the day-to-day grind, sometimes the choice that best advances the kingdom will be obvious, and sometimes it will not. When we reach a point where the two options have equal potential for building the kingdom, we ought not to be paralyzed by trying to pick the "right" one. Success in the kingdom of heaven is doing "whatever we do" because it brings glory to the name of our Lord Jesus. So long as we maintain our focus on the King, we cannot help but walk into those God-glorifying and joy-producing works that he has prepared in advance for us.[308]

I would love to close this book by telling you that grand things will happen to you and through you as you learn to make the kingdom of heaven your singular and preeminent reference point. We have many examples in Christian history of great things that God has done through his people—miraculous healings, ends to

---

[308] Ephesians 2:8–10.

injustices and poverty, and countless souls won to Christ—but none of that is guaranteed. God's methods and timing are inscrutable and do not depend on our abilities or good intentions.

Success for us is faithfulness to our call. We bear God's image and encourage others to submit wholeheartedly to his rule. We go out into the world as salt and light. We preach the good news of God's kingdom to the poor, bind up the brokenhearted, proclaim freedom for the captives and release from darkness for the prisoners, comfort those who mourn, and provide for those who grieve.[309] God works in us and through us to bring justice and truth to the nations.[310] As Christ's body on earth, we become fathers for the fatherless and defenders for the widows.[311]

So long as we, with God's mercy, maintain a singular focus on Christ, we do have his promise that "he will make our righteousness shine like the dawn"[312] in a dark and broken world. The world will experience God in our words and our lives. His sheep will hear his voice and gather 'round. Believers will humbly encourage each other on to new heights of righteousness, mercy, justice, integrity, and doctrinal correctness.

Yet, even as God's people clamor around us to encourage us and bear us up, the world, with its broken institutions made up of fallen humans, will hate and abuse us, as it did Jesus before us. Many of us will be counted worthy to suffer and even die for our faith. This, too, is for our good and God's glory. In being overrun for Christ, we will find that we have, in reality, overcome the world and been given a place among God's people in the kingdom of heaven.[313]

When we have begun to live out the gospel where we are, then we need to keep going. Some should stay to continue raising up new disciples, but many, if not most, should physically move on to new mission fields. We can start by reaching out to nearby

---

[309] Isaiah 61:1–2.

[310] Isaiah 42:1.

[311] Psalm 68:5.

[312] Psalm 37:6.

[313] Matthew 5:10.

neighborhoods and communities and by breaking through the glass walls separating resourced and under-resourced communities here in our nation and in our churches. Others of us will need to go further still, crossing oceans and continents to find any and every place where God's love is not known in word *and* deed.

As you leave this book and continue to weigh your life and your options, I pray that now, more than ever, you would not be distracted by the details. What will you do or wear or eat? Where will you go? Whom will you go with? How will you get there? Forget about these questions, for there is only one choice in life. Who (or what) will sit on the throne of your life? Every other decision is simply an opportunity to take a step toward or away from your preeminent reference point.

So, what will it be for you today? Life or death? God's kingdom first and alone or your own kingdom with its various distractions?

Appendices

1

Apostles' Creed[314]

I believe in God, the Father almighty,
　creator of heaven and earth.

I believe in Jesus Christ, his only Son, our Lord,
　who was conceived by the Holy Spirit
　and born of the virgin Mary.
　He suffered under Pontius Pilate,
　was crucified, died, and was buried;
　he descended to hell.
　The third day he rose again from the dead.
　He ascended to heaven
　and is seated at the right hand of God the Father almighty.
　From there he will come to judge the living and the dead.

I believe in the Holy Spirit,
　the holy catholic church,

---

[314] *Ecumenical Creeds and Reformed Confessions* (Grand Rapids, MI: CRC Publications, 1988), 7. This creed was not produced by the apostles themselves but does contain their teachings in what is arguably the most condensed form. This creed dates back to the fourth century.

the communion of saints,
the forgiveness of sins,
the resurrection of the body,
and the life everlasting. Amen.

2

The Richly Dwelling Word

Let the word of Christ dwell in you richly as you teach and admonish one another with all wisdom, and as you sing psalms, hymns and spiritual songs with gratitude in your hearts to God.

—*COLOSSIANS 3:16*

Christianity is built upon the teachings of the apostles and prophets, with Jesus's teachings serving as the chief cornerstone.[315] These teachings are preserved for us in the canon of Christian scriptures. To build on this foundation we must know it and respond to it. When it comes to Scripture, Jesus taught that there are really only two responses: obedience or disobedience.

Therefore everyone who hears these words of mine and puts them into practice is like a wise man who built his house on the rock. The rain came down, the streams rose, and the winds blew and beat against that house; yet it did not fall, because it had its foundation on the rock. But everyone who hears these words of mine and does

---

[315] Ephesians 2:19–22.

not put them into practice is like a foolish man who built his house
on sand. The rain came down, the streams rose, and the winds blew
and beat against that house, and it fell with a great crash.

—MATTHEW 7:24–27

In their simplest form, the teachings of the apostles, prophets, and
Jesus are simply the good news of redemption. This is the story of
creation, de-creation, and re-creation that we walked through in
part one of this book. If we are to build on this foundation properly,
it is imperative that we be letting the words of Christ dwell in us
richly. Here are a few pointers for getting to know Jesus better
through his Word:

- *Keep a regular, dedicated study time.* Every day we are
  inundated with false values and images of success.
  To combat the lies in our belief system, past and
  present, we will need to intentionally make time to
  be in God's Word. The more regular and the more
  frequent this time is, the better for renewing our
  minds. If you have never done this before, try starting with twenty minutes every day. Pick a book of
  the Bible, like one of the gospel accounts, and read
  through it. Make sure to aim for a time of day that
  fosters consistency and a location that keeps distractions to a minimum.
- *Read the whole book.* The Bible is a long book. It
  can be tempting, because of the length, to read the
  first few pages, a couple more in the middle, and
  then skip to the end. While this may work for some
  books, the Bible is not one of those books. Every
  part of it, including the ancient history lessons and
  seemingly boring genealogies, is God breathed
  and, therefore, useful for training us in godliness.[316]

---

[316] 2 Timothy 3:16–17.

If we only ever jump around, we end up ignoring certain parts of the Bible and opening ourselves up to great imbalance in our beliefs and in our practical expressions of godliness. To avoid this mistake, consider using a reading plan that takes you through the whole book over the course of a year or two. Your church may have these plans, and they can also be found online. Daily study Bibles are also available.

- *Understand it before you apply it.* As with every book, each verse in Scripture was written in such a way as to convey a specific meaning to its immediate audience. Sometimes that meaning is plain to us (with the help of translators) thousands of years later, and sometimes, because cultures change and languages evolve, the meaning is not so plain (even with a good translation). Only after we have gotten at the original meaning can we begin to decide what the verse has to say to us today. One of the most important steps in that process is recognizing the very different genres within Scripture—Old Testament narratives, psalms, gospels, parables, apocalyptic revelations, and so forth—and how that affects the way each passage should be read, understood, and applied.[317]

Remember, the Word of Christ does not merely dwell in us; it does so richly, bearing returns in our lives and those around us. Where our lives do not agree with Christ, we must submit ourselves to be taught, rebuked, corrected, and trained by his words. We renew our minds with his truth. Everything in life is defined by its relationship to Jesus Christ, not by our vague human perceptions or concretely pragmatic sense of how things ought to

---

[317] For more on getting to the original meaning of the text, I recommend *How to Read the Bible for All Its Worth* by Gordon D. Fee and Douglas Stuart (Grand Rapids, MI: Zondervan, 2003).

be. His Word is the lamp that lights our way[318] and the anchor that keeps us from being "blown here and there by every wind of teaching."[319]

So, with the Spirit's help, we need to put away our agendas and our baggage. We must fight the urge to get defensive when Scripture strips our sinful nature bare. We must also resist the desire to propose questions whose only purpose is to stave off the need for immediate change. For the new life in Christ to take root and thrive, our old lives must be done away with. We need to trust our Heavenly Father in his pruning.

As God's children, we have a wonderful promise. His law (i.e., his will of desire) is not only written down in Scripture for us, but as we read it and meditate on it, the Holy Spirit is writing it on our hearts as well.[320] As Paul puts it:

You show that you are a letter from Christ, the result of our ministry, written not with ink but with the Spirit of the living God, not on tablets of stone but on tablets of human hearts.

— 2 CORINTHIANS 3:3

As love letters from Christ to a broken world, we tell his story by saying the things he said and doing the things he did. We admonish one another with all his wisdom and teach others to obey everything he commanded. We offer his praises to anyone and everyone, starting with our neighbor and continuing on until the nations have heard of the wonders of our God. In short, we build up the body of Christ by training up those already within the fold and by inviting those who are not yet with us to join us as we worship the one true King.

---

[318] Psalm 119:105.
[319] Ephesians 4:14.
[320] Jeremiah 31:33.

3

A Model for Prayer

Devote yourselves to prayer, being watchful and thankful.

—Colossians 4:2

The life of a disciple is one of unbroken communication with King Jesus.[321] We seek him regularly and frequently in the Bible, and we also freely converse with him. Unlike the hierarchy within earthly kingdoms, subjects of the kingdom of heaven are not only allowed but also expected to be in constant contact with the King.[322] Though in our sin we could not look upon God, let alone talk to him, because of Jesus's work we can now approach his throne of grace with confidence.[323]

Prayer is for our sake, not God's. He knows what we need and what we will say, but he wants us to demonstrate daily our singular

---

[321] Here in Colossians 4:2, the NIV misses here the notion of *continual* devotion to prayer, but see also Romans 1:9–10, 1 Thessalonians 5:17, and Ephesians 6:18.

[322] Devotion to prayer was modeled by Jesus, the apostles Peter and Paul, and the early church (Acts 1:14; 2:42; 6:4).

[323] Hebrews 4:16.

dependence on him. In demonstrating our helplessness, we are giving free rein to the power of the Spirit in our lives and in the world around us. The Spirit does not need our permission to act, but he often waits for our acknowledgement of need before he will do the things he longs to do in and through us.[324]

Scripture has a great deal to say about how we should pray and what we should pray for. Prayer is between believers and God. It is done in isolation and in concert with other believers.[325] Fine-sounding words are not necessary, as our audience is God and God alone. With the Holy Spirit inside us, mere groans from our hearts are prayer enough to be heard and answered by our God.[326]

Still, it is worth noting how Jesus instructed his first disciples to pray:

> *This, then, is how you should pray:* "*Our Father in heaven, hallowed be your name, your kingdom come, your will be done on earth as it is in heaven. Give us today our daily bread. Forgive us our debts, as we also have forgiven our debtors. And lead us not into temptation, but deliver us from the evil one.*"

> *—MATTHEW 6:9–13*

Volumes can and have been written about this simple, meaty prayer. However, we will only examine a few of the basic elements of this passage. As we move through the prayer, it will be helpful to compare it to our own. The question we can ask repeatedly is this: Are our prayers marked by the same kingdom focus?

To those of us who fiercely guard our independence, notice the plurality of the prayer's first word, "our." Instead of praying for ourselves alone, true disciples pray on behalf of the whole body of Christ. Whether we are praying out loud, in the isolation of a room with the door shut, or sitting in a church pew, we remain one with

---

[324] James 4:2.

[325] Matthew 6:6; Matthew 18:19.

[326] Romans 8:26–27.

the rest of his body. Our attachment to the community of believers is so strong that we cannot pray for ourselves without simultaneously interceding on behalf of our fellow saints.

From the outset, it is also obvious that God is the focus of prayer, and preserving his name from defamation and obscurity is our primary concern. Thus, making much of God is not simply something we do for the benefit of others; it starts in our private dialogue with him as we pray, "Our Father in heaven, hallowed be your name." The delight we find in giving his reign preeminence in our lives leads us to pray that his kingdom come (as evidenced by his will being done) in the lives of those around us as well.

Only God can follow God's will perfectly. Thus, the prayer that the Father's will be done on earth as it is in heaven is the prayer that humans would set the Son on the throne of their hearts and experience the indwelling of the Spirit. It is a reminder of the nature of the heavenly kingdom, which has broken in on earth. As we have seen before, this kingdom is only in the hearts of men and women whose lives have been brought under God's rule.

In the second half of the prayer, the needs of the body are brought before its head. While we are probably quite familiar with the idea of bringing our requests before God, it is worth noting that the language here, "Give us this day our daily bread," is unlike most requests we make in our day. It is too limited for our tastes, asking only for what is necessary to carry on with a life of kingdom proclamation. No plea is made for safety, comfort, luxury, or convenience. Nor is there mention of enlarging our territories or adding to our material wealth.[327] Perhaps this is because, as James

---

[327] See the prayer of Jabez in 1 Chronicles 4:10. This is a great example of why it is important to understand the genre of the book we are reading. Historical narratives like 1 Chronicles should not be read with a monkey-see-monkey-do mindset because they are descriptive, not prescriptive. In other words, they tell us what happened but not necessarily what ought to have happened. God did grant Jabez's request, but this is evidence only that God is good enough and powerful enough to accomplish his purposes even in the midst of man's selfishness.

notes, such self-focused prayers have no place within a heart fixed on Jesus.[328]

Just as the prayer began with putting God in his proper place in our hearts, it ends with the humble recognition of our ongoing helplessness to fight sin on our own. The words "forgive us our debts" are to serve as a constant reminder of the condition of our hearts. There is no room for self-righteousness or pride in the prayer of the disciple. We do not thank God for our goodness like the Pharisee, but throw ourselves upon his mercy like the tax collector.[329] In our debt, we find cause for humility and overwhelming gratitude.

God is not the only one being sinned against. To a *much* smaller extent, we, too, will be lied to, cheated, and stolen from. Others will abuse us physically and otherwise. Covenants we have made with others will be broken through no fault of our own. Thus, we are mindful, even in our prayers, of our need to forgive. Lack of forgiveness for others hinders both our prayers and our salvation to such a degree that forgiveness must be granted to our brother before any conversation with God can be sought.[330]

As disciples, the awareness of our tendency to sin is so keen that we pray against even the presence of temptation. We know too well the truth of the line from the great hymn, "Prone to wander, Lord, I feel it, prone to leave the God I love."[331] So we pray for deliverance, not from pain or suffering, but from being overcome by evil and lost forever in hell. We can pray in confidence that we will be "self-controlled and alert" against the evil one—our enemy who "prowls around like a roaring lion looking for someone to devour"—for we know that "the God of all grace, who called [us] to his eternal glory in Christ...will himself restore [us] and make [us] strong, firm and steadfast."[332]

---

[328] James 4:3.

[329] Luke 18:10–14.

[330] Mark 11:26.

[331] "Come Thou Fount of Every Blessing," words by Robert Robinson.

[332] See 1 Peter 5:8–10.

One of our more harmful practices in prayer is to use it as a means of determining God's will of direction, which is to say his specific will, for our lives. Instead of being content to seek first God's kingdom—fixing our eyes on him, putting sin to death, putting on Christ, and teaching others to do the same—and letting the details be added on accordingly, we make the details our primary concern. In doing so we paralyze ourselves with questions God has no intention of answering directly (e.g., What job am I supposed to have? Where am I supposed to live? Am I supposed to marry?).

When we learn to use the kingdom of God as our reference point, we can do away with any need for confirmatory omens like "open doors" and "the peace of God." Not only can we stop praying for these things, but as we learn to adopt our King's otherworldly values, we may begin to realize that many of the doors that once looked closed are in reality opportunities for perseverance and overcoming to the glory of God. Likewise, we may realize that the sense of peace, which we relied on to tell us that we were in the right place, was the satisfaction of our earthly ideals of convenience, efficiency, and comfort.

God has told us through his readily available Word to concern ourselves *only* with expanding his rule in our own hearts, as well as those around us. Beyond that, we are to rest in his promise to take care of the details. Our purpose in prayer, as Jesus demonstrated in the garden of Gethsemane, is not to glean from God a new way of doing things. Instead, we pray that we would have the grace to perform what he has already shown us to do.[333]

---

[333] Matthew 26:36–44.

4

Our Common Commission

Then Jesus came to them and said, "All authority in heaven and on earth has been given to me. Therefore go and make disciples of all nations, baptizing them in the name of the Father and of the Son and of the Holy Spirit, and teaching them to obey everything I have commanded you. And surely I am with you always, to the very end of the age."

—MATTHEW 28:18–20

Christian discipleship is the cultivation of singular, wholehearted love for God in another human. Only God can cause the kind of spiritual growth that we seek, but he has given us the awesome responsibility of planting the gospel seed, watering the plant that sprouts from it, and pruning that plant so that it becomes increasingly fruitful.[334] Making disciples is how we, through God's grace, fulfill our default calling to fill and subdue the earth with the glory of God's kingdom rule.

---

[334] 1 Corinthians 3:5–8.

The process of making disciple starts deep within us as we submit ourselves to being discipled by another Christian and works itself outward until every aspect of our lives is submitted to our King in such a way that it best reflects his glory. As we are learning to love God with our whole heart, soul, and strength, we are passing on our preeminent love to others, beginning with our children (if we have any) *and* spreading it to our neighbor and eventually "to the ends of the earth."[335]

To be discipled and make disciples, as we have seen before, is the responsibility of every Christian. While we can be assured that Jesus does not expect all of us to quit our day jobs and leave our families to follow a stranger around for years at a time, there are still certain nonnegotiable elements that must be included in our discipleship if we are to fulfill the great commission of our King. Though other elements could probably be added, consider the following nonnegotiable characteristics of Christlike discipleship.[336]

Intentionality

Intentionality is the purposeful arrangement of life's details— the where, what, if, how, and when of everything—to encourage the expansion of God's rule in our own lives and in the lives of those around us. This may sound too programmed, and therefore unspiritual, but it is exactly how Jesus operated. Everything he did and said was aimed at doing the will of God the Father.[337] Even as Jesus called his disciples, for example, he did not do so under the pretense of becoming their worldly friend. Instead, he told them that his aim was to make them fishers of men who would catch new subjects for the King.[338] As fallen humans for whom godliness will never arise spontaneously, we must be all the more conscious and

---

[335] Acts 1:8.

[336] Though the names and organization have been switched around, I owe much if not all of this list to the works of Eric Russ, *Discipleship Defined*, and Robert Coleman, *The Master Plan of Evangelism and Discipleship*.

[337] John 8:28–29.

[338] Matthew 4:19; Mark 1:17.

intentional in how we use our interactions and relationships with others to shine Jesus's otherworldly light back on him.

Focus

Perhaps one of the less intuitive aspects of Jesus's intentional expansion of God's kingdom was his decision to focus his efforts. Though his ultimate aim was for men, women, and children from every nation to bow before him, he chose only a handful of men to pour his time and energy into teaching. Jesus did preach to the crowds, but as Pastor Eric Russ notes, we have something to learn from his particular treatment of his disciples.

> *He chose them out of a crowd in order for them to realize they were part of his inner circle. He wanted to be closer to them than He was to the masses. He taught them things that He had not taught the others. He was especially vulnerable with them. He trusted them with information to which no one else was privy...*
>
> *Christ's model, coupled with His exhortation to obey, shows that those who follow Christ will be developing {similar} relationships with others for the purpose of spiritual multiplication.*[339]

The beauty of focus is that it allows ordinary Christians, with ordinary jobs and responsibilities, to develop the depth of relationship required for the transformation from earth dweller to citizen of heaven. Even healthy believers, with their hearts and minds fixed on the proper reference point of God's kingdom, take a considerable amount of time to train to the point where they are able to live out, communicate, and multiply their faith. As we begin to take steps toward discipling others, it will be helpful to start small, with one disciple, for instance, and make sure our schedule can adequately accommodate any additional disciples before we start to meet with them as well.

---

[339] Eric Russ, *Discipleship Defined* (XulonPress, 2010), 58.

Commitment

For discipleship to achieve its goal of multiplying God's all-of-life-encompassing rule, it will require commitment to persevere over time and through differences, both personal and doctrinal. Time is required for at least two reasons. First, sound doctrinal understanding must be achieved before a disciple can pass along anything of worth to others.[340] Second, practical godliness is a process that requires much trial and error, with constant reexamination and refocusing of our thoughts, words, and deeds to better image the glory of our King.

To confound the matter, all manner of social, educational, and economic barriers may stand in stand in the way of spiritual growth. For example, if we expect our disciples to study God's Word, it will be helpful to ensure that they can read and possess basic study habits. Likewise, if we want them to work and provide for themselves and their families, we will want to ensure that they have the necessary skills to secure a job, including proper education, the ability to assemble a resume, knowledge of where to look, and understanding of how to conduct themselves in an interview and at work.[341]

Differences between disciplers and disciples will also inevitably arise. Where Scripture takes a clear stance, we must both align ourselves with God's Word. Failure to do so, no matter how devastating the truth is to our current lifestyle, exposes an unteachable heart that is not fully submitted to the King and thus not fit for discipleship. In this case, the discipleship relationship should be abandoned until such a time as teachability is recovered. Where no clear Scriptural stance exists, we must still spur one another on toward kingdom-first living. While the details of the gray areas are negotiable, the end goal of our efforts is not.

---

[340] 1 Timothy 1:3–7.

[341] One practical implication of this reality of barriers is that in areas where poverty is common and such barriers are high, discipleship takes longer and requires more peripheral resources to bring a person to the point of reproducible godliness.

Vulnerability

Despite our differences, we must approach discipleship with vulnerability, which is the honest desire to know someone and be known by them. As Eric Russ points out, vulnerability goes beyond simply giving others the statistics of our lives.

> We can be honest with someone without being vulnerable, able to restate the facts but unable or unwilling to share how the facts make us feel. This is where vulnerability finds its home.

> Being vulnerable is never about restatement of the facts; it's about letting people into the heart and emotions of the situations that transpire in your life. Vulnerability allows people to see that you are human. This is where true intimacy begins, when you stop being the only person that knows your heart by letting others into it.[342]

Others cannot ever ask enough questions to expose all of our sinful tendencies or faulty assumptions, nor should they have to. If we want to grow, then we must take an active role in being discovered just as we are and not as we want others to perceive us. Remember that our earthly nature is indeed *ours*, and we need to take ownership, in the power of the Holy Spirit, for putting our heart before the pruning shears of God's people.

Balance

In many ways, godliness is a balancing act. This does not mean balancing God with other important pieces of life, because that is idolatry. Rather, the balancing act of godliness consists of ensuring that God's glory is flowing through every available avenue of our image bearing. It does us no good to be one-dimensional Christians or, worse yet, one-dimensional churches. We must embrace the totality of our call as image bearers, and we must teach our disciples to do the same.

---

[342] *Discipleship Defined*, 59.

All of us have relative, if not absolute, strengths and weaknesses. If left to ourselves, we naturally gravitate toward an emphasis of our strengths, as evidenced by strong doctrinal churches like Ephesus or strong service-oriented churches like Thyatira. We often do the same thing on an individual level, training our disciples in *our* areas of strength rather than training them holistically. If we do not intentionally plan in times to train our disciples in the study of God's Word, prayer, and practical ministries of service and evangelism, then we will end up multiplying one-dimensional believers who look a lot more like us than they do Jesus.[343]

Reproducibility

Balance, in essence, allows for reproduction of Christlike Christians, which is, of course, the goal of discipleship. Jesus intentionally sought out and poured into a select group of disciples so that they would become fishers of men and reproduce themselves in generation after generation of discipleship. So it is for us. Countless generations of disciples separate us from Jesus, yet we, too, are to teach our disciples to obey everything he taught in word and deed.

Whether we begin with our child or our neighbor, the process of making disciples looks the same. As we are going about our Jesus-first lives, we invite others to join the kingdom of light, which has broken into our dark, sinful, and hopeless existence. With Scripture, we teach our disciples to fix their eyes on Christ through the essential truths of the Christian faith. His commands become their daily bread, and our lives become the living proof of God's mercy. In us, our disciples get a breathing, thinking, acting, and speaking example of a living sacrifice, in whom sin is constantly being put to death and Christ is constantly being put on.

After a time of training, we ask them to go and do likewise. Again, the goal is always in-kind multiplication. Disciples are expected to make disciples who are expected to make disciples who are expected

---

[343] While it is true that we are members with unique qualities and unique spiritual gifts, it is also true that these are given to augment and not replace our basic call to balanced image bearing.

to make disciples, and so forth. Reproducibility of key elements is vital and requires tireless reiteration, in word and deed, of the same message in every generation so that, whether it be the second, third, fourth, or one-hundredth generation, each disciple is teaching his or her disciples all the same things that Jesus taught the first disciples.

Fellowship

> Let us hold unswervingly to the hope we profess, for he who promised is faithful. And let us consider how we may spur one another on toward love and good deeds. Let us not give up meeting together, as some are in the habit of doing, but let us encourage one another— and all the more as you see the Day approaching.

> —HEBREWS 10:23–25

The importance of fellowship in the development of the believer is hard to overstate. The church is not a building, nor is it even a group of people that magically appears for a few hours every week only to disappear when the doxology has been said and the pews are emptied. No, the church is the same body and kingdom that we have been talking of all along. It is the community of singularly focused disciples that shines forth otherworldly light in the Monday to Saturday grind, just as readily as it does during a corporate worship service on Sunday.

The body is of utmost importance to the life of its individual members. We need the body to bear us up through our broken sinfulness and to spur us "on toward love and good deeds." While our common calling as humans is to bear God's image, we must realize that our image bearing is incomplete if we attempt to do it on our own. If our aim is to show others Christ, then we must invite them to experience him in his body, where his "fullness" can be found.[344] See how Coleman describes the revelation of Christ in the daily life of the early church.

---

[344] Ephesians 1:23.

In their community life, Christians developed an atmosphere conducive to growth. Questions could be asked and issues clarified without intimidation. Mutual trust existed. Whether in organized group meetings or informal friendly fellowship, the church translated theory into practice. To a remarkable degree, truth was demonstrated in real life. What they said and did was an object lesson in reality.

Nowhere was this more pronounced than in the beginning steps of persons just coming to Christ. These spiritual babes were immediately surrounded with love and made to feel a part of the family circle. No one could feel left out. Here was a community in which all shared the bonds of an everlasting covenant.[345]

Not only do we seek out the body for our own sustenance and the preservation of Christ's witness, we also do so for the joy that comes from fellowship with other believers. Look again at the description of the early church in Acts, but this time notice the emotions and attitudes of the first Christians.

They devoted themselves to the apostles' teaching and to the fellowship, to the breaking of bread and to prayer. Everyone was filled with awe, and many wonders and miraculous signs were done by the apostles. All the believers were together and had everything in common. Selling their possessions and goods, they gave to anyone as he had need. Every day they continued to meet together in the temple courts. They broke bread in their homes and ate together with glad and sincere hearts, praising God and enjoying the favor of all the people. And the Lord added to their number daily those who were being saved.

—ACTS 2:42–47

In spite of all the reasons the folks in the early church had to not get along, the men and women described above truly enjoyed being

---

[345] Coleman, *Evangelism,* 63.

close to one another! What made their fellowship so effortless was their delight in seeing others find the greatest joy of all in the King. If we have ever been part of a close-knit team, family, or local body of believers, then we may well have experienced this reality for ourselves. Delight allows people to seek each other out early and often during the course of a week, no matter how busy or complicated their schedules may be. The early believers "had everything in common," sharing resources, meals, homes, worship, travel, and ministry. Though their example is hardly a line-by-line recipe, we have much to learn from the attitudes and behaviors of the early church. As Coleman writes:

> In our stress upon carefully ordered public services and organized campaigns, we may overlook the basic apostolic ingredient of fellowship. Times have become more complex with passing centuries, surely, but the principle of association never changes.
>
> However structured, we must relate closely with one another. There are ways this can be encouraged in the regular worship services, even in formal, sacramental settings. Auxiliary meetings offer other opportunities for fellowship, especially small-group gatherings. In this connection the Sunday School provides many options. Emphasis must be given to the home and family in the program. Through it all, personal relationships need continual cultivation in the ongoing discipleship process. [346]

It may be hard at first, but we must not give up on learning to delight in our fellow believers. At the same time, we must fight to remember our mission to our neighbors still outside of the body. We need to balance our kingdom-building efforts by intentionally expanding God's kingdom from both within the body, where existing believers are spurred on to new heights of love, and from without, by offering those still wandering about in darkness the

---

[346] *The Master Plan of Evangelism*, 63–64.

Light that brings life to the lost. Joy-filled fellowship is wonderful, but it is not the end.

A Life of Discipleship

Most of us are probably unfamiliar with this kind of Christlike discipleship. The thought of giving ourselves so regularly and intentionally to yet another Christian activity may seem unrealistic. Our hesitancy is, at least in part, due to the fact that as average lay Christians we tend to see ministry as something entirely separate from our daily lives and more the business of pastors, missionaries, and other professional clergy. As Coleman writes:

> *The establishment of professional clergy has had a sharp effect on the average unordained Christian. The creation of such roles has tended to confuse the priesthood of all believers and has nullified the sense of responsibility for ministry. Many Christians feel quite satisfied with the situation, content to allow paid clergymen and staff do all the work. But even those who are more sensitive to their calling and want to be involved may experience a sense of frustration as they try to find their place of service. "After all," they may ask, "if I'm not a preacher or missionary or something of the kind, how can I be properly engaged in ministry?"*
>
> *The answer lies in their seeing the Great Commission as a lifestyle encompassing the total resources of every child of God. Here the ministry of Christ comes alive in the day-by-day activity of discipling. Whether we have a "secular" job or ecclesiastical position, a Christlike commitment to bring the nations into the eternal Kingdom should be part of it.*[347]

Everything we do in life is intentionally aligned to support our preeminent and common call to both observe and pass on Christ's rule. While this may sound exhausting, this is the only way to serve

---

[347] *The Master Plan of Discipleship*, 10–11.

Christ without burning out. The call to give King Jesus *everything* is only overwhelming when we are trying to hold onto *something else* at the same time. When we let go of the things that hinder us, we soon realize how light a yoke and easy a burden the Christ-first life truly is.

Selected Bibliography

(Listed in order of appearance)

J. I. Packer. *Concise Theology*. Wheaton, IL: Tyndale House, 1995. Electronic version available from Logos Bible Software 4.

A. W. Tozer. *The Pursuit of God*. Harrisburg, PA: Christian Publications, 1982.

Mark Driscoll and Gerry Breshears. *Doctrine*. Wheaton, IL: Crossway, 2010.

John Piper. *For Your Joy*. Minneapolis, MN: Desiring God, 2009.

C. H. Spurgeon. "Christ Is All." Sermon published on February 18, 1915, delivered at the Metropolitan Tabernacle, Newington. Access date October 16, 2011. http://www.iclnet.org/pub/resources/text/history/spurgeon/web/ss-0016.html.

Lee Strobel. *The Case for Christ*. Grand Rapids, MI: Zondervan, 1998.

C. S. Lewis. *The Weight of Glory*. New York, NY: HarperCollins, 2001.

John Piper. *Desiring God*. Sisters, OR: Multnomah Publishers, 2003.

Dietrich Bonhoeffer. *The Cost of Discipleship*. New York, NY: Touchstone, 1995.

C. S. Lewis. *The Screwtape Letters*. New York, NY: HarperCollins, 2001.

Elisabeth Elliot. *Shadow of the Almighty*. New York, NY: HarperCollins, 1979.

John Perkins. *Let Justice Roll Down*. Ventura, CA: Regal, 1976.

Michael O. Emerson and Christian Smith. *Divided by Faith*. New York, NY: Oxford University Press, 2000.

David Brainerd. *The Life and Diary of David Brainerd*. Edited by Jonathan Edwards. Peabody, MA: Hendrickson, 2006.

Kevin DeYoung and Greg Gilbert. *What Is the Mission of the Church?* Wheaton, IL: Crossway, 2011.

Robert Coleman. *The Master Plan of Evangelism and Discipleship*. Peabody, MA: Prince Press, 2000.

Robert Lupton. *Theirs Is the Kingdom*. New York, NY: HarperCollins, 1989.

Gordon D. Fee and Douglas Stuart. *How to Read the Bible for All Its Worth*. Grand Rapids, MI: Zondervan, 2003.

Eric Russ. *Discipleship Defined*. XulonPress, 2010.